Innovative Lean

A guide to releasing the untapped gold in your organisation to engage employees, drive out waste, and create prosperity

Andy Brophy

and

John Bicheno

PICSIE Books, 2010

Innovative Lean

Published by

PICSIE Books

Box 622

Buckingham

MK18 7YE

United Kingdom

Copyright © PICSIE Books 2010

Publication date: March 2010

ISBN 978-09541244-8-9

British Library Cataloguing-in-publication Data

A catalogue record for this book is available from the British Library

This book is dedicated to the life and memory of

Mick Brophy (1942 – 2008)

Mick lived his life guided by first-rate principles which

were grounded in Respect for People

Book Navigation

This book is intended to be a practical guide to give direction to both leaders and practitioners on setting up an Idea Management System in the workplace. Even though the book assumes a basic grounding in the philosophy of Lean it is not solely intended for use by those familiar with Lean. All workplaces from every business sector can benefit from applied creativity and employee driven innovation. Hence the glossary in the appendix provides details of the Lean terms discussed throughout the book and this should help readers new to the world of Lean. It is hoped that this text will become a dog-eared and highlighted manual on the desks of employees in organisations from all sectors. Idea Management Systems have massive potential whether you work in a manufacturing plant, a hospital, or indeed any office or workplace.

It is recommended that readers begin by reading through section one which gives a good grounding and overview of Idea Management including the potential of the concept and discusses some surprising aspects of this technique. The book can then be read in any order. For those wishing to get straight into action, section two details the support infrastructure and provides a guiding roadmap. It must be stated that there is no one best way to implement the system and you may or may not decide to use all of the recommended steps and tools. Cut your coat according to the cloth as it were, and adjust to align with your own unique culture. Section three gives an outline of the structure for running an accelerated idea workshop. This is a useful consideration if you need an intense focus on a burning issue or at the launch of the system to demonstrate the potential. Section four works though some of the accessories that make for a physically conducive creative environment. It also details some recommendations on how to nurture a creative and innovative culture to cultivate top performance of idea systems. Section five describes twenty resources for breaking out of habitual thinking patterns. This is an especially useful gift to employees both as a profit generating set of tools and as a suite of personal life skills. Finally in section six it's the "rubber meets the road" stage where eight real life case studies of Idea Management Systems from the manufacturing and hospital domains are explored in a question and answer format. There is no substitute for real life lessons. In the appendix, four distinguished experts in Idea Management share snapshots of their expertise. The appendix also contains an audit for rating the effectiveness of the Idea Management System, and a list of 30 ways to improve personal creativity. There is a macro audit for determining the current state of play of the organisation's creativity and innovation performance. This is a useful tool to give a business a baseline at the outset of their journey and to demonstrate the gap opportunity.

Contents

Acknowledgements

Acknowledgements

There are several people we are indebted to for help in completing this book. A special thanks to Anthony Denatale of ideasUK for the visit to their organisation and for the research advice and numerous contacts generously given. To all the organisations that either hosted us during the research or who provided phone interviews. These include: Jayne Garner, Rob Bland, and John Duddy from Ricoh Products, Allan Kemprett from Larsen & Shaw. Thanks to Jim Schwarz for the numerous insightful conversations. Gratitude is also expressed to Alan Robinson for the enlightening chats. Sincere thanks to Chuck Yorke for the comprehensive review of the Technicolor TIPS System. Thanks to Bernie Sander for his extensive advice and for the provision of the PiT Stop accelerated idea generation workshop. Bradley Willis formerly from Toyota provided a wonderful overview of Toyota's fantastic method of harvesting employee ideas. Jack Simms for the wonderful overview of the Dana idea system, thanks to you. Three case studies are included that showcase the wonderful pioneering examples of the power of idea systems in hospitals. Firstly we thank "Lean Hospitals" author Mark Graban for connecting us with John Burns of The Children's Medical Center in Dallas and to John for sharing their engaging journey to date. Joseph McCrory representing The Baptist Health Care organisation provided an inspiring overview of their prolific idea system. Thanks to the creative trio at Virginia Mason in Seattle; Jennifer Phillips, Alisha Mark, and Diane Miller for sharing the wonderful story of the medical centers Everyday Lean Ideas system.

The Front cover:

The large picture in the middle of the front cover portrays a small water droplet rebounding on hitting the water surface. The energy from the impact is dissipated as a series of ripples spreading across the water. This is a good analogy to describe the impact of employee ideas; small ideas implemented consistently over time have a great ripple effect. They can be put into practice rapidly and spread many times across an organisation. They allow the release of employee's potential energy, just like the single water droplet dispels its potential energy extensively.

The golden brain is shown inside one of our employee's heads. Is one of the reasons that we fail to engage people in the creative use of their potential that we cannot see their amazing brains, or forget? The light bulb represents an employee idea and the hand represents innovation which means that we implement the ideas brought forward. We see a nurse to remind us that idea systems are applicable to all sectors, notably in environments as critical as hospitals where the situational knowledge of the people on the front lines is so critical to harness in terms of improving patient outcomes.

The "best places to work" slogan and the acorn perhaps sum up the essential aim of idea systems: to engage your people through involving them in decision-making and workplace improvement, which in turn leads to their growth and development.

Chapter 1   Lean and Ideas

Opportunity for improvement lies all around.

For centuries, women in rural Africa have carried water in pots from rivers and wells to their homes. Often, this is a daily task taking several hours. And, yes, it is the women not the men who do this onerous work. The women found that the easiest way to carry the pots was on their heads, buffered by a blanket or scarf. This is still the widespread practice today, carried on by thousands if not millions of women. But in 2009 a new innovation appeared. A 40 litre drum, rotating around its axis, with padded strips around the circumference, is pulled along by hand like a cart using a handle attached to each side of of the drum. Overnight, productivity quadrupled and physical effort was halved. Appearance of the drums has been greeted with scenes of wild enthusiasm. Simple? Brilliant? Why did it take so long?

Throughout the world, water usage is becoming a limiting factor. As standards of living increase, more and more people would like to use a flush toilet. And what should be done immediately after using the loo? Wash your hands. What happens to the water used when hands are washed? So, why not use the hand wash water to help flush the toilet next time? Astonishingly, after billions of flushes, this simple idea is only now being developed.

These two ideas went unnoticed by millions of people for decades. The best ideas are often the most simple.

So it is with Lean. Perhaps the greatest success of Lean has been the ability for everyone in the organisation to begin to "learn to see" waste. "Wear your Muda spectacles" says Dan Jones. But, of course, you cannot just announce that, henceforth, everyone needs to identify and reduce waste. It simply will not happen. It needs a method, a procedure, a system to surface problems, and opportunities and a methodology to gather ideas and to implement them. And all this will only happen in an environment, a culture that encourages ideas. The pre-requisite, as Deming said, is "Drive out Fear". Easier said than done! This can only happen with consistent, long-term, demonstration. Actions speak louder than words.

Steve Spear explains the rise of Toyota by drawing two intersecting straight lines, with different slopes but both moving from bottom left towards top right. The lines represent performance or productivity in the auto industry. Toyota starts low but ends highest. Others (GM?) start higher, but grow more slowly. There is no "silver bullet" explains Spear. It is just the cumulative difference in speed of innovation and implementation of many, many small ideas. In short, it is about cultivating, harvesting and implementing the ideas of almost everyone, and not relying on a few ideas by productivity "experts". If everyone is sensitised to the possibilities, if everyone is an "industrial engineer", you have a formidable enterprise.

As Thomas Cochrane says, "Lean" is what you become, not what you are. This is like fitness. (Elias, 2008). You are never 100% fit. Being "fit" for one activity does not necessarily mean you are "fit" for other activities. Fitness is a lifestyle thing, much of it mental, not a one-off visit to the gym. The "tools" that are used need to be appropriate – weights, aerobics, long distance runs or swims against sprints and getting out of the blocks fast, diet or adding bulk, and so on. Ideas may be universal, but they need careful adaptation.

Yes, Lean is about the compound effect of many small ideas. But harvesting big ideas is also important. Cisco recently held a competition amongst staff, with a $250,000 prize for the best breakthrough idea. A group of senior managers spent four months full-time going through the ideas. An extensive thought-through process was put in place on the submission of ideas, to ensure that all but the winning idea remained the intellectual property of submittors. Staff were allocated to develop and refine the business case of ideas with good potential. One could imagine that, with such a substantial prize for the winner, there may have been many dissatisfied participants. Apparently not. The real points of the exercise were getting the intellectual juices going, the realisation of the potential of people in the company, and refining the idea management process.

Lean is about doing many small things, but it is also about stopping doing things. It is easy to add things, but subtracting may be a better thing to do. Take the example of the removal of traffic lights and street furniture and signs in parts of Holland. Doing so resulted in, perhaps counter-intuitively, better traffic flows and greater safety. Pareto's Law says that perhaps 20% of customers account for 80% of profits. But if 80% of the work generates 20% of the profits, can we stop doing some of that 80% and re-focus to the more profitable end?

Five Lean Principles and Ideas

Womack and Jones in *Lean Thinking* (1996) set out five Lean Principles: value, value stream, flow, pull, and perfection. These have served all those who seek to implement Lean very well. All, of course, are beacons for ideas. In the intervening period, Lean has expanded massively into non-traditional areas – healthcare, services, local and central government, defence, prisons, to name just a few. Perhaps, therefore, it is appropriate to re-cast the five principles, even though this is probably presumptious. The proposal for the revised 5 is:

1. Purpose

Stand back and ask about what the system is there to do. There may well be several stakeholders each with different, valid aspirations. (Example: A Prison: Rehabilitation or punishment?) For ideas, the "purpose" question should be asked at various levels as the overall purpose or purposes are deployed throughout the organisation. Are we in the "drills" business or the "holes" business? Are we selling cosmetics or are we selling "hope"? For ideas and improvement, "purpose" is a most potent concept.

2. System

A system is more than the sum of its parts. Like a human, or an airplane. The holistic concept is more important than the parts. An airplane comprises parts that have no aspirations to fly – just the opposite, in fact! And it is the system in dynamic interaction with its environment that enables it to survive and prosper. An airplane without sufficient forward movement crashes. A system has feedback, both positive and negative, that enables it to adjust. A flying airplane continually makes adjustments to changing conditions, or it falls. So many improvement ideas will need to relate to these and other characteristics – total system improvement, not sub-system improvement; interactions between parts; adjustment to a changing environment; end-to-end; dynamic not static;

and feedback. The idea of a "value stream" remains a powerful concept in Lean, but sometimes does not capture the essential characteristics found in, for example, service.

3. Flow

Flow is at the heart of Lean. Flow is concerned with lead time reduction, end-to-end. As Ohno once said, "All we are trying to do is to reduce the time from order to cash". Remember this clever statement – it is not just about manufacturing operations. So, keep it moving. "It" is the focus of the purpose - the product, the patient, the customer, but not the machine or the worker". Never delay the customer by an activity that has relevance to the organisation but not the customer. Don't waste his or her time. (Womack and Jones, 2005.) Mackle talks about "creating flow, maintaining flow, organising for flow, and measuring for flow". To this can be added Design for flow, Supply for flow, Distribute for flow. (Mackle in Bicheno, 2006.) Note that we are not talking tools here – like a "House of Lean". We are saying that there should be focus on identifying and eliminating all the barriers to flow. This would include understanding demand and bottlenecks. Demand is of two types – value demand and failure demand. The latter results from errors or omissions in your own system, and should be eliminated. (See Bicheno, 2008.) Organising for flow means redesign of the value streams end-to-end, probably using what Womack calls a "value stream architect" who has the cross-functional vision. Maintaining flow includes all activities for sustaining and improving flow. Measuring flow should also relate to end-to-end measures, particularly the cumulative time to respond to customer requirements.

Of particular relevance for ideas and improvement is an appreciation of Kingman's equation, simply expressed as $L = TUV$. Lead time is a function of process time, utilisation, and variation. This is a non-linear function, as shown. Note that "variation is the enemy". If we ignore variation (and sometimes we do by drawing a simple value stream map), we conclude that lead time is simply the sum of the process times. This is totally unrealistic except at very low rates of process utilisation. (Utilisation relates to the ratio of load to capacity.) At higher utilisation, variation causes lead time to explode. There are two types of variation – demand variation, and process variation. So it is the interplay of utilisation, demand variation, and process variation that is critical. What are the ideas to reduce variation? Can utilisation be improved without the negative consequences? Yes, by reducing failure demand and by improving capacity by taking out waste (especially at bottlenecks; capacity comprises work and waste, said Ohno.) Put it another way, and $L=TUV$ is a neat encapsulation of the three crucial aspects of the Toyota system – Muda, Muri, Mura – waste, 'overburden' (or utilisation), and variation. Kingman's equation is justifiably called the Equation of Lean. Ideas that smooth demand, reduce failure demand, reduce waste, and reduce variation will all improve flow and reduce lead time.

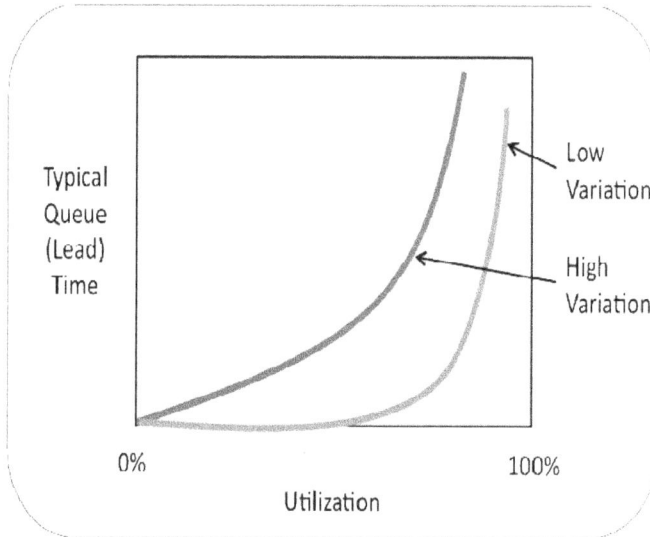

4. Perfection

Perfection is an aspirational goal, that all should strive for. It has internal and external dimensions. Internally it is about zero defects, six sigma or better quality, and ever-higher process capability. It is about variation, mistakes and complexity (Hinckley, 2000). Reduce all three by attention to all 6 'M's of the fishbone diagram: Men / People, Machines, Materials, Methods, Mother Nature effects, and appropriate Measures. This gives 6 x 3 = 18 cells for ideas. Externally, perfection is about zero defections (of those customers you value), and about enhancing the total customer experience. Thus, internally we can use a process map, and externally we can use a "service blueprint" to track a customer's "moments of truth".

The Six Sigma DMAIC, or Deming's PDSA, are established improvement cycles that need to relate strongly to ideas. The cycle is discussed below.

5. People

Last but by no means least, comes the true engine of Lean. Lean has been, and continues to be, a revolution and a revelation with respect to the use of people. No longer are "bring your brain to work", and "people are our most important assets" meaningless, hollow cliches. An organisation where everyone contributes ideas will be both more effective and more efficient than an organisation that relies on the select few. Efficient certainly. But effective? Yes! Take IKEA, an organisation founded on the observation that it is difficult to move furniture in your car. Hence the idea of flat packs.

Mahesh and others have spoken of the "Pygmalion Effect". This effect is now beyond doubt. Thus, for example, if one group of schoolchildren is continually told that mathematics is difficult and useless, and another group is continually told and shown that mathematics can be fun, is widely used and, like a computer game, is challenging and rewarding – the difference in eventual mathematical ability will be marked. This study has been replicated many times. Another study showed marked differences with Israeli recruits. Instructors were told that one group had special ability and the other not when in fact there was no difference. The instructors reported vastly different outcomes. In industrial and service settings, several studies have shown similar results. (See Ariely, 2008, Mahesh, 1993)

Liker says, *"Lean systems will degrade without ongoing improvement from every single employee through a myriad of simple, quick changes. What brings Lean structures to life is people – people engaged in continual improvement"*

System degradation is the natural state. It is called Entropy and is the Second Law of Thermodynamics. It applies to Lean as much as it does to all natural systems.

Many companies find that the biggest test during their Lean transformation is engaging employees in the daily habit of continuous improvement. 40 years ago Taiicho Ohno recognised how vital this is – he stated that "the heart of TPS is management's commitment to empowering employees with the daily practice of continuous improvement". This is what an Idea Management System can deliver if structured and supported properly.

Ohno said that the essence of TPS is developing within each employee a "kaizen consciousness" (opportunity awareness). TPS experts view Lean transformation as changing the thought process of every employee. Becoming Lean to them is about improving organisation performance, seeing problems, solving them the right way, and in doing so continually increasing the intellectual capital and skill of all members of the organisation. Tapping and evolving the creativity of every employee, if properly cultivated and directed, has unlimited potential.

But, note, Ohno's "kaizen consciousness" is not just doing occasional, or even frequent, kaizen events between which times no improvement takes place. The Entropy principle show us that doing nothing means you will be slipping back. Ohno intended to mean improvement by everyone, every day. This means a continual flow of ideas, nearly all of them very small but having large cumulative effect. A "kaizen consciousness" is a "mindset thing".

Management should strive to see the oak in the acorn; that is, endeavour to develop people to be all that they can be.

Vision, Ideas, Filters, Implementation, Communication and Culture

1. Communicate the vision

The ability to visualise and articulate the future state for an organisation is vital. Toyota has a phrase for this long-term vision – "True North". The vision or purpose should align and energise the entire workforce. It should connect with our emotions; we are driven by emotions not reason. Vision or purpose is the essence of what the organisation is delivering. This must be instilled into every level of the organisation and be utilised as a source of inspiration for improvement ideas. It becomes the magnet to set in motion the energy for congruent ideas. This clarity of purpose is not achieved overnight; hence we need to develop and filter ideas quickly (ideally self-filter) to support the vision.

Section One

It is no good having ideas about improving activities that should not take place at all – that are part of an inappropriate system design – unless the ideas are directed at removing such activities entirely. Hence the need for clear vision or purpose.

It is management's prime task to foster improvement. That means continually communicating the vision or direction, encouraging a questioning attitude, ensuring that movement towards the vision takes place, removing barriers, and insisting on testing assumptions, ideas, and hypotheses.

2. Generate ideas – continually, not in batches like kaizen events

Idea activity needs to develop into an "everyday ideas" practice. Instil the mindset of the tortoise versus the rabbit. The rabbit makes progress in quick bursts but sleeps frequently along the race, so much in fact that he loses the race to the tortoise with his slow but persevering pace.

Regular kaizen events are positive, especially at early stages of Lean implementation, but should not have the effect of batching ideas whilst waiting for the next event.

Idea submission needs to be made easy. No complex forms or procedures. Make it visible. Perhaps use an idea white board or small cards that move through the stages of implementation. Get the idea out in the open, and develop the detail later.

Often, it will not be good enough to sit back and wait for ideas. The flow of ideas may be meagre. So, ideas will often need to be focused on a theme – like improving customer experience, reducing delay, cutting weight, improving safety, or finding new customers.

3. Filter good and inappropriate ideas fast, and give feedback

Clearly, the generation of ideas from everyone can give huge competitive advantage. This is necessary but not sufficient. Ideas need to be filtered – good from inappropriate. At the same time, bureaucracy must be avoided.
Filtration needs to be done in such a way that it does not discourage further ideas. Indeed, even inappropriate ideas should be viewed positively as evidence that people are thinking about improvement. Encouragement may lead to a string of valuable ideas later. An unsuitable idea also brings opportunity to develop the employee. Why did they not know that their idea would be unsuitable? And some inappropriate ideas may be the seed for a valuable idea, because they have at least uncovered an opportunity.

4. Implement good ideas, fast, and give recognition

The most powerful and effective motivator for future ideas is recognition and implementation.

Not implementing an idea fast feels the same as rejecting an idea. Maybe worse – if insincerity is suspected. Show the progress of implementation on a board – perhaps using a Plan Do Study Act cycle or an Idea, To Do, Doing, Done visual.

Thought will need to be given as to how to implement low cost, high return ideas almost immediately with the minimum of fuss and delay - perhaps decentralised budgets for this purpose. Indeed, this point, and points 2 and 3, all suggest that idea management needs to be as decentralised as possible.

It is said that Toyota has a greater than 95% implementation rate for ideas as many of them are not implemented in their original form, but are enriched with the employee.

Recognition needs to be compatible with the culture of the organisation, but bear in mind the ample evidence against large individual monetary rewards. Most ideas originate with a person but are developed and implemented by a team. Recognition, always starting but not necessarily ending with a simple 'thank you', needs to reflect this.

5. Communicate and spread ideas to other potential benefactors

The fifth element is to communicate and spread good ideas around the organisation, to other areas where the idea may be applicable. Otherwise it is wasted potential. This is a huge challenge, with two sub-problems. First, to identify (or self-identify) the area where the idea may be useful. Second, overcoming the 'not invented here' syndrome. Hence, 'roll in' rather than 'roll out'; self-discovery rather than imposition.

Thought will need to be given to spreading ideas, ranging from a measles chart showing the location of ideas to data base solutions.

6. Create a culture for all this to work well

And finally, a management style or culture that fosters, or better insists on, the first five happening. As is so often the case with Lean implementation, success depends on both top-down and bottom-up effort.

An example: say someone has the idea that to make in a big batch is a good idea. After all, it may save the "waste" of changeover and improve yield while adjustments are made. Do we simply accept and implement the idea? Of course not! Easy for a person well versed in Lean to understand that this would be counterproductive. But not necessarily easy for the idea suggester to accept. Worse, out-of-hand rejection, may "turn that person off", causing resentment, and possibly discouraging the person from making a real breakthough idea next time around. The best way to prevent this is by "Socratic Engagement": Don't just reject the idea out of hand (or worse, don't give any reaction – just forget it) but talk it through by asking questions. "What would a large batch do to the delivery of other products?", "What will that do to total inventory holding?", "What happens if the whole batch is found to be defective?", "What happens if the forecast is incorrect?". This must be genuine talk-through, genuine dialog including listening, not questioning merely to disprove. In fact, there may be a situation where a large batch IS warranted!

For questioning to be effective there must be clear vision of the ideal state. Is the idea moving us towards that ideal? This is one of the most challenging areas for management – to communicate the vision. Note: This is explicitly not setting "stretch goals" or KPI's for next year! It is Toyota's True North, The HP Way, The Apple vision of a beautiful, friendly machine, South West's vision of low cost but fun.

If the vision is clearly understood by all, a filter device is not required. Ideas will self-filter. That is an ideal in itself, possibly approached by Toyota. But for many, a degree of filtering will be required.

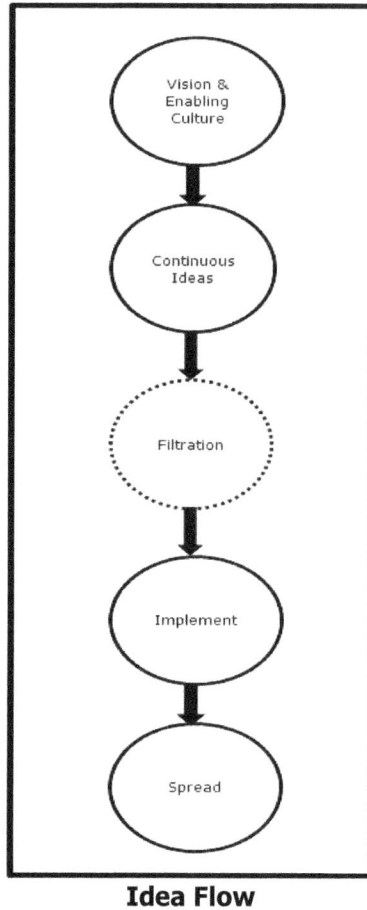

Idea Flow

The Barriers to Ideas

Front-line people have always had ideas about the work. Why? Because they are at the Gemba all the time. So what have been the barriers? Probably five: Respect, Communication, Support, Tools, and Fear.

- First, recognition, belief, and respect. Do senior managers really believe, in their hearts, that "lower ranks" and front-line operators can make significant improvements? This cannot just be said; it must be demonstrated until it becomes embedded. A major reason for management participation in kaizen events is not the skills that they bring to the event, but what they take away with them in the form of lessons learned about the good ideas and insights that come from their people. In short, respect and humility are the starting points.

- Second is communication. One of Steven Spear's Four Rules of Toyota DNA is "one clear communication path". Often front-line people know the issues and the problems, but senior management does not. Somewhere there is communication breakdown. And communication needs to be appropriately rapid, like the human body's nervous system that handles minor local variation locally, but communicates more severe changes such as burns immediately to the highest level. As with the human body, a break in the upward communication chain can be disasterous. An idea may be a symptom of local malfunction that, like disease, if caught early enough can be stopped, but if ignored can prove fatal.

- Third is support. The image of the inverted triangle is appropriate. Is everyone focused upwards, attempting to satisfy the demands of the management apex? Or is the triangle inverted where all levels are focused on the base and are there to support and faciitate front-line operations?

- Fourth is appropriate tools and methods. People may have ideas but some ideas will need development and refinement. Other aids and training may be required to help recognise opportunity. In Lean, every tool has a dual purpose – the use of the tool itself, and as a way of highlighting problems and opportunities. Example: 5S is for housekeeping and variation reduction, but is also to highlight workstation opportunities when everything is not in its place.

- Fifth is fear. Perhaps most important of all. None of this will work if there is fear. "Drive out fear", Deming said. Most employees will not admit to fear, but the idea of fear should include the fear of being ignored, rejected or criticised. Many employees are "watchers" who continually monitor the reaction of managers at all levels, and act accordingly. Fear also extends to the stealing of ideas. The first idea stolen by a manager from an associate is the last idea that will be put forward by that associate.

Waste, Problems, and Ideas

We need ideas to reduce waste and address problems. But first, what is "waste" and what is a "problem"? Lean practitioners know that waste is anything that does not add value from the customer's viewpoint. Would the customer be prepared to pay for the activity? If not, it is waste. And there are three types of activity: value adding, non-value adding and pure waste activity. This definition is useful and proven. But an alternative is to say that waste is any activity that does not directly contribute towards meeting the primary purpose of the system. And the primary purpose should never be just to "make money" or to "create satisfaction". Those are measures or proxies for the prime purpose.

In service business, a prime waste is "failure demand". Failure demand is caused by not doing something or by doing something wrong. It results in delay and rework either soon after or, worse, much further along the end-to-end value stream. Like a plumber arriving at a house without the needed parts or requiring a customer to re-sumbit forms and details.

And what is a "problem"? In Lean, a problem is not necessarily a "big thing", like a major constraint. No, it is anything that is out of place or unexpected. So standard work that is not being followed indicates a problem. Why is it not being followed? Is there a better way? Perhaps the standard is a top-down imposed, inappropriate standard rather than a standard developed by workers in response to a need. Or, maybe the standard is fine but the people are just not following it for some reason. So, every "problem" is an opportunity to find out, to explore. In short, a new idea is needed. Learning is the essence of improvement.

This explanation of what a problem is, leads to two strands. First, Deming spoke of the "94/6" rule. About 94% of problems lie with the process, and only 6% lie with the people running the process. So, don't blame the person first, but first seek out opportunities in the process.

Second, Deming, and more latterly Steven Spear have written about experimentation and the scientific method. Deming, following Shewhart, wrote about Plan, Do, Study, Act. Yes, we all know about PDCA or PDSA. But maybe not! Steven Spear in *Chasing the Rabbit* tells what PDSA really means by recounting the methods of Admiral Rickover of the US Navy's Nuclear Propulsion programme. The programme has now had 5000+ vessel years of accident free operation, whilst their Russian counterparts have had numerous accidents. How so? It began with the modest recognition that there is a great deal that is unknown about nuclear propulsion in operating conditions and that therefore there is a need to uncover areas of ignorance. This is done by predicting, in advance, what the characteristics or outcomes of any and every process or study will be. Then the actual study outcomes are compared with the prediction. Where they do not match, this reveals areas of of incomplete understanding, which must be pursued. These are problems, where ideas will be required. In other words, this is scientific method properly applied. Simple - but so infrequently done. If a pipe bursts, don't just fix but seek the root cause. The common management approach is seldom to predict and seldom to reflect. The "quick fix" of the pipe is not the cause of the burst, so it may recur. Spear says that Toyota methodology is similar - slowly but persistently building a "community of scientists" from top to bottom, with a questioning culture. The crucial steps are prediction beforehand, that looks forward, and review afterwards, that looks back on the prediction and probes for the reasons for the gap. "What have we learned?" is the vital question. This is not just having ideas, it is testing them.

Some managers claim 30 years of experience. Good for them - if that is the case. But, some of those of those managers, who have not explicitly or implicitly adopted this PDSA methodology, do not have 30 years experience – they have one year 30 times!

So, it is not just a problem that is an opportunity but an identified gap in knowledge that is an opportunity. Steven Spear talks about creating the ability to be continually surprised. Surprise is the essence of discovery and hence improvement. This, Spear believes, is a characteristic of great "Rabbit" organisations that bound ahead of the pack. One can create surprise by setting out expectations or forecasts and then looking back to see if that forecast was correct, and if not, why not? Rabbit or hare???
Spear says anyone and everyone can do this. It is more of a mindset. But it is a mindset that does not tolerate muddling through, and re-inventing the wheel.

Russel Ackoff, who died in October 2009, spoke of three approaches to problems. Let us illustate with reference to a frequently recurring stock-out problem.

First, "resolving problems". This is where a solution is worked out by consensus – often at a meeting. Perhaps the participants vote on the solution. The group gathers and brainstorms ideas on the causes of the stock-out. Then they work out a solution by consensus. Perhaps they decide to review the stock position once per day instead of once per week. This gives production a few more days to schedule completion of the order. It leads to an improvement.

Second, is "solving problems". Here a more scientific approach is used. Perhaps some Six Sigma tools are envoked to improve the forecasting, and revise the safety stock levels. An early warning trigger is established to dynamically change the safety stock and reorder point. This method relies more on quantitative modelling and analysis, and less on discussion and consensus.

Note that both of these approaches may involve tradeoff or compromise. But, in Lean, you strive for perfection, not compromise. (In the Russian TRIZ methodology, this is referred to as the "AND" solution rather than the "OR" solution. We want to have our cake AND eat it.)

And, finally, there is dissolving problems". Here, the "problem" is made to disappear. Dissolving problems requires a wider or system perspective. We look for root causes and problem clarity. In the stock-out problem, the need is for appropriate, minimum levels of inventory. What are the barriers? Infrequent, slow response. Why? Because replenishment is in batches. Why so? Because of long changeover times between making batches. So, what can we do about changeover? Reduce it! How? By SMED analysis. And what ideas do we get from our initial analysis? Reduce adjustments, and reduce the "scavenger hunt". It would help if we had more warning. Ideas for these? Standardised settings, welding a spanner to a nut, a changeover trolley, a kanban signal. So, ideas come out from a hierarchy of questions, but beginning with an understanding of purpose.

TRIZ and Problem Solving

Discovering a problem and its root causes doesn't always give us the ideas we need to find a solution. Brainstorming is commonly used in problem solving teams to get to solutions. It is designed to release a team's thinking from past patterns and unearth ideas that people might have unconsciously blocked. However brainstorming doesn't always work. If the resolution lies outside the knowledge of the team, this method won't reveal it. This is often compensated for by bringing in outsiders or "wildcards". This can work if their fresh perspective is what the team needs.

Brainstorming is subject to psychological inertia. Psychological inertia refers to the combined constraints of perceptions, past experience, current knowledge, common sense, and cultural norms of a team. This tends to lead the problem solvers down traditional routes, while the solution may lie far outside this path of inertia. TRIZ does not give the team the detailed design solution, but it points the team in focused and clear directions for solutions. But because the TRIZ methodology is based on technology, not psychology, even non creative individuals can capitalise on the power of TRIZ and create breakthrough solutions in a short time.

TRIZ was developed by Genrich Altshuller from patterns he analysed when reviewing hundreds of thousands of patent applications. From this he discovered that there were 40 Inventive Principles behind all of the inventions that were ever discovered.

A partial list of some of the 40 Inventive Principles includes:

- Moving to a new dimension (use multi layers, turn it on its side, move it along a plane etc.)

- Self-service (make the product service itself, make use of wasted energy)

- Changing the colour (or make it transparent, use a coloured additive)

- Mechanical vibration (make use of the energy of vibrations or oscillations)

- Hydraulic or pneumatic assembly (replace solids with a gas or liquid, join parts hydraulically)

- Use porous material (make the part porous or fill the pores in advance)

- Use thermal expansion (change to more than one material with different coefficients of expansion)

- Copying (instead of using the object use a copy or projection of it)

- Thin membranes (use flexible membranes, insulate or isolate using membranes)

- Regenerating parts (recycle), use a composite material

This is a powerful list; just reading them can generate ideas.

The reason TRIZ works so effectively is the simple fact that over 90 percent of the underlying generic problems product and processes encounter today at a given organisation have already been solved at another company or even in a completely different industry—perhaps even for entirely unrelated situations—using a fundamentally different technology or approach.

Once the real problem (conflict or compromise) is identified, it is converted from an industry-specific problem to a generic problem by shaving away the subject matter. In TRIZ, generic problems have generic solutions. The team will then explore the generic solution paths to create an industry-specific solution. An example of a specific problem might be how do we dry clothes faster, the abstract generic problem would be how do we separate a liquid from a solid.

TRIZ applies to both continuous improvement and new innovations because continuous improvement requires solving current problems, and innovation requires finding ways to solve customers' problems.

TRIZ is divided into five main elements:

Contradictions

TRIZ aims to eliminate problems rather than accepting compromises. There are two kinds of compromises or contradictions:

Technical contradictions: when something gets better, something else gets worse. An example would be; making a product stronger and more robust (good), but the weight increases (bad). TRIZ doesn't depend on the team to solve these problems. They are solved using the 40 principles of problem solving.

Physical contradictions: are eliminated using four basic principles to separate the requirements that appear to be contradictory in time, space, between the parts and the whole, and between the wider system, system and sub-systems. For the latter an example for preventing machine tool crashes could be a wider system sensor (poka yoke) that tracks the relative positions of each tool and adjusts if the risk of collision is imminent.

Ideality

TRIZ urges problem solvers to begin with the Ideal Final Result and work backwards, rather than moving forward from the current state. The idea of "free, perfect & now" or "self" – self monitoring is the aspirational goal.

Functionality

Understanding function and functionality at the most basic is fundamental to successful application of breakthrough methods. Solutions change, but functions stay the same.

Value Engineering, a wonderfully powerful and often forgotten industrial engineering methodology, can be combined with TRIZ to blend a potent improvement methodology. Value Engineering is a systematic and creative effort that analyes the functions of products or processes to ensure that required functions are achieved at the lowest possible overall cost. A good functional analysis will help a team identify value mismatches, which are instances where a disproportionate amount of cost is allocated to an area of low customer interest.

Resources

TRIZ encourages making the best use of any resource that is not being used to its maximum potential. Common improvement resources that can be our friend include thinking three dimensionally about space (above, surface, and below ground) and using gravity to save energy.

Space, Time & Interfaces

Effective problem solving requires appreciation of how a system is affected by spatial, temporal and interface issues. Don't just think about the current state in the present, but also about the past and the future. As mentioned above it is useful to also consider the wider system, system and sub-system. This gives 9 boxes for understanding and projection.

Don't Band Aid Problems

Lean puts emphasis on "root cause" problem solving. When a road gang reaches an area requiring repair, a good Lean thinker would ask why the pothole(s) have appeared in the first place. They learn to look around and question. For instance, are the potholes due to flash flood (a special cause), or to simple wear out (common cause), or to increased road usage (could this have been predicted?). It is a wasted opportunity simply to go out and repair, and not to learn. Good Lean thinkers treat every problem as an opportunity to learn. Doing so opens up a whole raft of new ideas.

SAB Miller calls this activity "when the bobby on the beat meets the body on the beach". First, look around and see if the murderer is running away. If so, go after him. But if not, collect the evidence before the tide comes in and destroys the evidence. This would mean recording relevant data for later examination, and ideas.

Six Types of Improvement

We have spoken about incremental, small scale improvement as in the stockout problem above, and about breakthrough, big scale improvement as at Cisco. These may also be referred to as "point kaizen" and "flow kaizen". Of course, these two overlap, but it is convenient here to think of them as two types.

Some ideas are obvious to front-line staff because they experience problems every day. They are at the Gemba. Other ideas arise out of experience at other organisations, through reading and discussion, and maybe through "eureka" moments. This may be termed passive improvement.

But other ideas arise from problems that need to be "surfaced". The iceberg analogy is appropriate. Problems are deliberately uncovered, by the methodology of "proper" PDSA that includes surfacing issues that are inadequately understood, as described by Spear's story of the US Nuclear Propulsion fleet. Other surfacing is done routinely by established Lean techniques such as inventory withdrawal, line-stop and andon lights, heijunka schedules that track production against pitch times or day-by-the-hour schedules, and by methods such as out-of-control conditions on a SPC chart. These may be termed enforced improvement. Having "no problem" is a problem.

Thus we have four categories for present operations. But then we would like to look at future operations. It may be too late to tackle some kinds of waste once the product has been designed or the facility has been built. But we can design new products and services to wring out waste at the development stage. So now we have six categories for improvement ideas. These are shown in the figure below.

IMPROVEMENT CATEGORIES

	INCREMENTAL 'Point Kaizen'	BREAKTHROUGH 'Flow Kaizen'	
EXECUTION			
PASSIVE / ENABLED	Suggestion Schemes Self Directed Teams Quality Circles Open Book Mgmt, 5S, Waste awareness	Industrial Engineering O.R. (Some) Six Sigma	
	TRIZ		
DRIVEN / ENFORCED	Line stop, Andon, Heijunka, Visual Mgmt, Inventory withdrawal, 'Chalk circle', Red Tags Six Sigma projects Kaizen events	Value Stream Mapping Supply Chain Development	
PREPARATION	DFM / DFA Group Technology Value Eng D.O.E.	TRIZ	
		3-D Simulation Location decisions Set based design Target Costing	

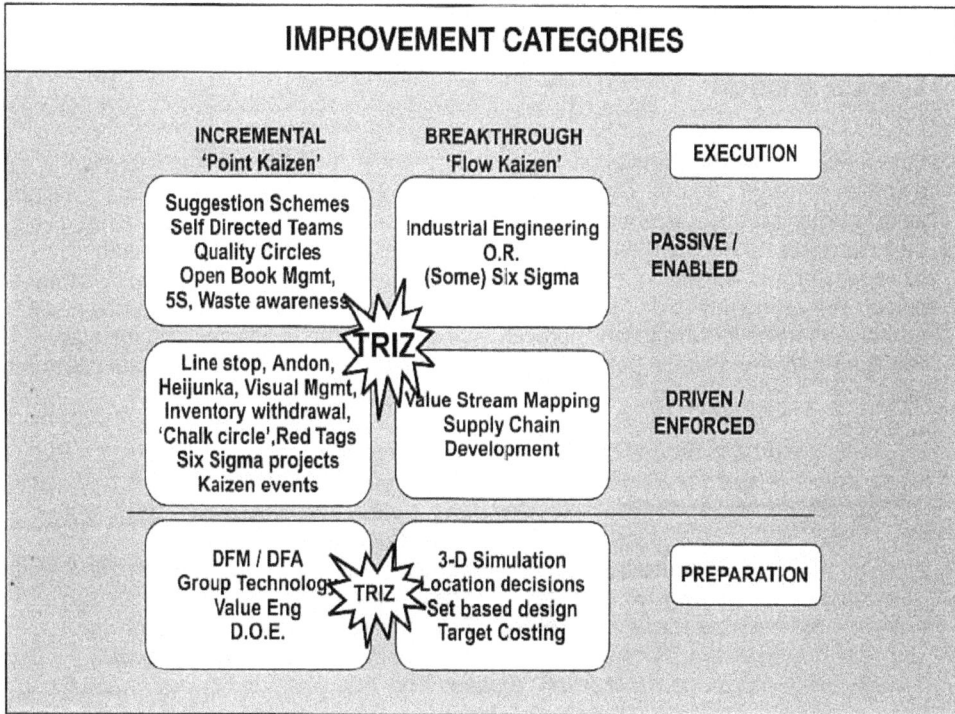

It is important that ALL SIX are used. A Lean organisation concerned with idea management needs to have policies for each of the six categories. An organisation also needs the "professional" improvers such as industial engineers, operational researchers, six sigma black belts, and TRIZ experts. But these people have no monopoly on ideas.

In each category, there are good ways to go about ideas and implementation, and not-so-good, even poor, ways. Generally, the latter have arrogance, lack of humility, lack of respect, at their core. The "professionals" need to work with the "real experts" who face problems every day. Rolling out solutions without involving employees is generally not a good idea – this smacks of arrogance, imposition and we-know best. Roll-in is much better. Here, people self-discover or joint-discover with the experts, each giving recognition to the others' unique capabilities.

Ideas alone are not sufficient. An idea that is lost through non-implementation, or that is not sustained, is perhaps the greatest waste. It may even be insulting!

So, let us begin...

Chapter 2   Idea Management Overview

Employees see problems and opportunities every single day in their immediate work areas that their managers do not. They observe with frustration and maybe eventually cynicism as their organisations waste money, and lose customers. When employees are not given the opportunity to be heard and the time to implement their ideas they lose faith in management and are thus not fully engaged in their work. Often organisations become so tied up in meeting day to day targets that they never take time out to "sharpen the saw". A system that delivers proactive improvements on a daily basis ensures that the saw remains sharp. The parable below describes a scenario that many organisations can surely relate to.

A young man approached the foreman of a logging crew and asked for a job. "That depends," replied the foreman. "Let's see you chop down this tree." The young man stepped forward and skilfully chopped down a great tree. Impressed, the foreman exclaimed, "You can start on Monday."
Monday, Tuesday, Wednesday, Thursday rolled by -- and Thursday afternoon the foreman approached the young man and said, "You can pick up your pay check on the way out today." Startled, the young man replied, "I thought you paid on Friday." "Normally we do," said the foreman. "But we're letting you go today because you've fallen behind. Our daily felling charts show that you've dropped from first place on Monday to last place today."
"But I'm a hard worker," the young man objected. "I arrive first, leave last and even have worked through my coffee breaks!" The foreman, sensing the young man's integrity, thought for a minute and then asked, "Have you been sharpening your axe?"The young man replied, "No sir, I've been working too hard to take time for that!"
Author Unknown

Idea Management is the discipline that enables the methodical capture, implementation, and sharing of ideas across the organisation. It can deliver continuous innovation, improvement, employee involvement, and up-skilling to the workplace. The primary concentration is on participation and skills development rather than on the monetary value of the ideas. What could support the company vision more than developing employees? The emphasis should be on encouraging everyone to make improvements. For employees, management's receptiveness to their ideas gives them a real chance to address many of the problems and opportunities they see on a daily basis, and henceforth make a personal impact on the performance of their organisations. Everyone's work becomes much more rewarding and less stressful. A steady stream of ideas can have a profound impact on an organisation's culture.

Idea management is an enabler to realising the true potential of an organisation. Well designed Lean systems continually flush out a myriad of hidden problems and opportunities that are restricting performance. Often nobody except employees on the frontlines can see these issues, as they are the people who face them daily. But frequently employees either do not have the skills or mechanism to resolve the issues. An effective Idea Management System can provide employees with both the skills and an infrastructure to solve the problems themselves.

Each year, Toyota's employees implement 1.5 million ideas that save the company over $300 million annually. Inspired by this a decade ago, the Chairman and CEO of Dana Corporation asked his 80,000 employees to submit two creative ideas per month and implement 80% of them. A cultural transformation began, and for over ten years Dana's employees implemented about 2 million ideas per year, saving over $2 billion. Beginning in 2001 by using the same process, Technicolor in Detroit with 1,800 employees generated 20,000 ideas, implemented over 12,000 of them, and saved the company over $10 million within a year.

(Bodek 2001)

Holistic Involvement

Some of the perils of improvement, in a organisation that still belives improvement to be the exclusive domain of "experts", "managers" or "white collar" staff include:

- It does not motivate the frontlines to participate, nor does it nurture their abilities and help them acquire new skills.

- Although large scale improvements are implemented successfully, little attention is paid to the many small improvement ideas that competitors cannot copy.

- Ideas that might lead to labour efficiency or cost reduction are often prioritised, even though they might not be of benefit to the employees.

- Improvements by professionals do not reflect the aggregate knowledge of people who are closest to the work. People naturally tend to resist ideas that are forced upon them, however take ownership of ideas that they help to develop and implement.

Many types of organisations, from manufacturing to hospitals, are now embarking on their own Lean journeys but are missing a vital ingredient to success - the need to get all employees comprehensively involved in improvement activities. Lean initiatives will disintegrate without this ongoing involvement from every employee contributing simple, quick everyday changes. There is a need to shift our focus from the traditional fire-fighting hero and take on the role of fire-preventer via proactive surfacing, searching and implementation of improvement ideas. A successful Idea Management System (hereafter known as IMS) engrains Lean and small continual improvement into the core of an organisation's values.

The IMS makes itself available as a problem solving resource. Surfacing problems is at the heart of the Lean philosophy as we continually strive to strengthen weak spots. Consequently a constant flow of problems, dictates that we need everyone in the organisation solving problems - not just the so-called "white collar" staff or managers. Team leaders take on a key role in coaching and mentoring associates to solve and coordinate the problems they expose. The front line staff will become more competent with each repeated cycle and a virtuous circle results. As more and more problems are raised and solved, employees grow in confidence and capability. One of the best forms of up-skilling employees is to provide a well run IMS to foster their personal development. The honest organisation would freely admit: "I do not know what my employees know" –

and herein lies the essence of the reason for the IMS, namely to make best use of the knowledge of all employees.

Gathering and harvesting employee ideas is not just about cost cutting. All service and manufacturing organisations incur two types of cost:

- Costs that deliver value to the customer. These costs are good and are to be welcomed and even increased if they help differentiate the organisation's offerings.

- Costs that are incurred, but don't end up delivering value to customers, are waste. An important type is failure demand. An IMS should be focused on dissolving these wastes thereby improving the performance of the workplace.

Many cost-cutting exercises don't distinguish between these two forms of cost, which is why many cost cutting efforts end up causing more destruction than good over the longer term.

History of Idea Management

Who knows when managers first used the ideas of their staff? An early recorded example in 1880 was William Denny, a Scottish shipbuilder, who asked his workers for advice on ways for building ships at lower cost.

Employee idea systems received a real boost during World War II. Companies were under pressure to produce larger quantities of goods with a scarce workforce and fewer resources. After World War II, Deming and Juran brought the concept of continuous improvement to Japan's beleaguered industrial complex. Here, employee ideas quickly became an important force.

In 1986 Imai first alerted the world to the Kaizen Teian (improvement proposal) system in his book *The Key to Japan's Competitive Success*. He mentioned "less well-known is the fact that the idea system was brought to Japan by the US Air Force and the TWI (Training Within Industry) program".

The Kaizen Mindset

Kaizen is one of those cherished concepts that is at once a philosophy, a principle, a practice, and a tool. Kaizen was developed in Japan following World War II. The word Kaizen means "continuous improvement". It comes from the Japanese words "Kai" meaning school and "Zen" meaning wisdom.

Kaizen is a system that promotes involvement from every employee - from upper management to the cleaning crew. Michael Ballé points out that Kaizen is concerned with developing the human capital (confidence, trust, and the knowledge) of the workforce. It's a deep commitment to helping employees reach their full potential. Everyone is encouraged to come up with small improvement ideas on a regular basis. This is not a once a year, or a monthly activity. It is continuous. In most cases these are not ideas for major changes. Kaizen is based on making little changes on a regular basis - always improving productivity, safety and effectiveness, and reducing waste. Kaizen involves setting standards and then continually improving those standards.

The Development of Idea Management

Traditional Suggestion Boxes

Suggestion boxes don't work, period. There is the story about the suggestion found in the suggestion box, "Can you get rid of the suggestion box? Nobody ever uses it!" Employees will feel they would be better off dropping their ideas into a paper shredder if they never hear about previously submitted ideas. A suggestion box may simply become a complaint box. Added to this is that traditional systems get stuck in their own bureaucracy. There are long implementation times, and high rejection rates partly because some are duplicate suggestions which have already been paid for. Cumbersome evaluation processes with flawed reward systems (see table below for typical characteristics of this system) can also be an issue. Most traditional suggestion systems fall prey to ideas for other people to do something, rather than the originator of the suggestion. Hence the system can become laborious (JHRA 2 1992). Why bury ideas away in a box? Bring out the ideas, discuss them, and implement them!

Kaizen Style Idea Management

The three primary aims of a Kaizen style IMS are:

1. **Participation** – The aim is to increase the sense of belonging in the organisation, leading to increased motivation and active involvement resulting in improvements.

2. **Training and Skills Development** – An IMS improves problem solving and kaizen ability, and also speeds up on-the-job training. Move away from the concept of simply harvesting ideas from the employees to a mechanism to improve, up-skill and develop people. Focus on the people and the results will follow. Improved trust and teamwork is an aim.

3. **Effect** – Kaizen results in both tangibles such as improved efficiency of operations, and reduced cost of poor quality, and intangibles such as improved safety, morale, and an environment that delivers trust and teamwork.

"Not everything that counts can be counted and not everything that can be counted counts". Albert Einstein

In contrast to traditional suggestion systems that are typically hierarchical in control and approval, the Kaizen method gives authority to associates on the front line with the supervisor acting as the catalyst and coach for ideas and managing the infrastructure for implementation. The focus is on the many small daily annoyances and minor problems that associates can resolve themselves and lead to a smoother shift. The intention is that problems are nipped in the bud prior to them escalating into bigger issues. Good Kaizen has high participation rates and the reward for the most part is associates having a say in running the business and seeing their ideas come to fruition.

Kaizen can be contrasted with the traditional suggestion box. Emphasis on employee involvement explains most of the difference between the two. Typically, financial returns are about ten times greater for kaizen than the traditional systems such as the suggestion box (Robinson & Schroeder 2004).

The table below contrasts the two systems.

Attribute	Kaizen Style Idea System	Conventional Suggestion Box
Objective	• Employee Involvement • Competency and Skills Development • Cost Savings and Avoidance	• Cost Savings
Emphasis	• Small ideas • Daily "nuisance" or "misery factors" workarounds • Waste elimination and prevention	• Large Ideas
Workforce Participation	• Typically > 50%	• Typically < 5%
Implementation	• Employees encouraged to implement their own ideas and/or co-ordinate implementation	• Usually by a subject matter expert
Reward and Recognition	• Intrinsic reward of seeing idea being used • Token recognition gift • Colleague recognition	• % of savings
Idea Approval Rate	• Near 100% (ideas are enriched)	• Approx. 25% (duplicate ideas are rejected as they're already paid for)
Evaluation	• Mostly by direct frontline supervisor	• Central Evaluation Committee
# of Ideas per Year	• Typically thousands • Target often is 24 per employee per year	• Typically a few hundred larger ideas

Comparison of main features of kaizen style and traditional idea systems

The Compounding Power of Small Ideas

"1% improvement in 1000 things, rather than 1000% improvement in one thing" Tom Peters

Many small everyday tasks are done imperfectly or even unacceptably; or are overlooked and forgotten about. Think of stained cutlery in a restaurant. Sweeping change takes place when hundreds or even thousands of small ideas are implemented. These miniscule improvements, when generated millions of times over, add up to an enormous improvement. It is when managers are able to get large numbers of small ideas that the full power of the Lean paradigm is unleashed. For the system to work, managers need to empower the workers and their immediate supervisors to manage the ideas.

Large ideas within idea originator's department that the supervisor doesn't have authorisation to implement	Large ideas outside idea originator's department that may need cross functional approval
(Target Quadrant) **Small ideas within the idea originator's immediate work area that can directly be implemented with the guidance of their supervisor**	Small ideas outside idea originator's department that are outside their scope of implementation authority

Primary Target Quadrant for IMS Ideas

"You don't fly up a hill. You struggle slowly and painfully up a hill, and maybe if you work very hard, you get to the top ahead of everyone else." (Armstrong 2002)

The implementation rate for improvements proposed by those closest to the problem is very high. This is because people enjoy carrying out their own ideas and are committed to seeing them work. It gives them a feeling of having a direct impact in the running of the workplace and a sense of accomplishment. Hence getting the person who raises the idea to implement it or to participate in implementation is crucial to the success of the system. This concept is the cornerstone of a successful system. This level of empowerment won't happen overnight and at the outset people may need support in implementing their ideas, but this investment will develop more capable employees over time.

Section One

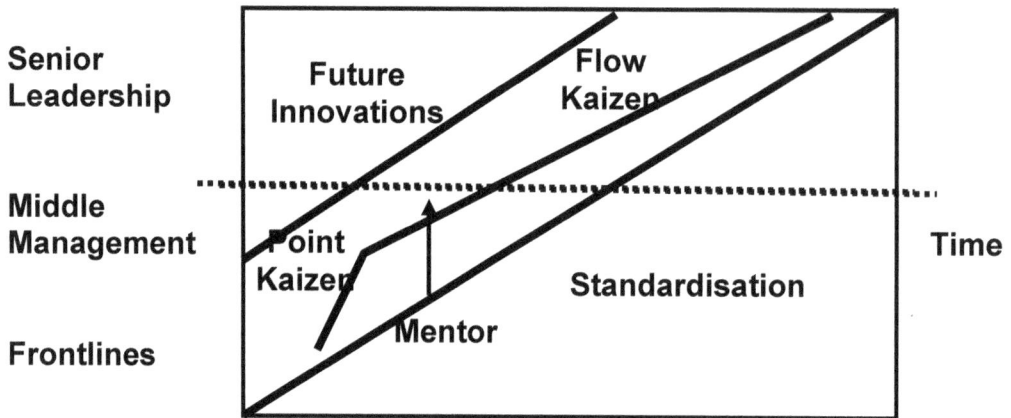

The figure above, adapted from Imai, shows four types of activity appropriate to a Lean organisation. The time spent on each activity by any level in the organisation is the horizontal distance from left to right, appropriate to that level. Standardisation is to do with "holding the gains" and establishing a platform for further improvement. Note that standardisation applies to all levels in the organisation – only the proportion of time varies. Mentoring is also an activity that applies at all levels. But mentoring is particularly appropriate at the front line. In the central band is Kaizen or continuous improvement which has two overlapping sub-types. Point kaizen is to do with local improvements and is generally associated with lower levels in the organisation. Flow kaizen is to do with larger improvements and is generally found towards the top right of the central band. But everyone is involved in Kaizen. Future developments and innovations are coordinated in the higher levels in the organisation.

A good idea system enables managers to concentrate on higher level innovations and future developments. However managers have responsibilities for today's work (Kaizen) as well as for fostering the future flow of ideas through mentoring. In Kaizen Philosophy, top management spend the majority of their time on future value creation and on current kaizen improvement work concentrated on making today's processes better for tomorrow. A smaller percentage of their time, perhaps 20%, is spent running the day to day operations and Gemba walking. Frontline associates spend the majority of their time running the day to day operations, but crucially 15-20% of their time should be utilised making small kaizen improvements. Hence they are both task doers and task improvers.

Cultivation of large improvements without the small ones has little or no effect on *changing the behaviours* that ultimately impact productivity and profitability. This is where mentoring is so important. Small improvements encourage change and are not disruptive. Most don't compromise ISO or FDA requirements. They are also less likely to migrate to competitors which therefore accumulate into substantial competitive advantage over the longer term. Remember that technologies and processes can easily be copied or bought. Implemented ideas cannot.

Small problems get neglected when you go only for the biggest "bang for the buck". Solve the small problems and you wouldn't have big problems (Hall 2006). The real reason for encouraging and implementing many ideas, however small, is to send out a positive message about improvement. To get the best ideas, you need all the ideas. This volume principle was what led Edison to his great innovations. The point is that you cannot predict when great ideas will emerge. Even if 95% of ideas are hardly worthwhile – at least from a cost-benefit viewpoint, the other 5% will more than pay for the whole program, and then some!

The IMS should be allowed to mature over time. In the early stages management can seek ideas that are very basic. This stage is to get employees involved, thinking about, and questioning their work. It also allows ideas raised to be implemented (as they are basic) and builds momentum. In the intermediate stage, management places emphasis on up-skilling so that employees can provide better ideas. In order for the workers to provide better ideas, they should be trained in problem solving and in the use of creativity tools. This requires education. The hidden benefit is that the work becomes much more engaging as people use their thinking skills on a daily basis. Ultimately, in the advanced stage, after the workers have become more educated, involved, and hence engaged, management starts to be concerned with the financial return on ideas.

One cause of failure of idea systems is announcing the system company-wide. If the message is taken to be sincere, a flood of pent-up ideas may result that can overwhelm the filtration system, however decentralised. Then credibility is lost, never to be regained. Roll-out is therefore an important consideration, bearing in mind the capacity to handle ideas. In early days experience and therefore capacity may be lacking. A pilot, followed by area by area deployment may be wise.

An alternative, or parallel activity, is to focus ideas on particular concerns like winning new business, paper reduction, weight (mass) reduction, or duplication. These also require careful consideration. A focus on aims such as general waste reduction, lead time reduction, or customer service may be inappropriately wide or vague especially in early days of an IMS. A focus on particular aims has the dual advantages of limiting the filtration effort but also of providing a stimulant.

Focus can be derived from the Lean concept of Policy Deployment or Hoshin Kanri. Good Policy Deployment deliberately focuses on a few key areas and deploys the aims for those areas level by level in a participative way known as "catchball". The "Whats", the "Whys" and the "Whens" are top-down from the top, but the "Hows", "Where" and "Whos" are proposed bottom-up at each level. So, why not focus idea management alongside policy deployment initiatives as a way of getting everyone involved. Team members, assisted and mentored by team leaders, then make improvements at all levels.

The Hierarchy of Improvement

Organisations ideally need to practice Kaizen at five levels:

Level 1: The Individual Kaizen (Kaizen Teian)
The individual needs to be the recognised expert of their own process. At the local workspace level there are always opportunities for waste reduction – work piece orientation, inventory, equipment location, work sequence, ergonomics, poka yoke, and so on. The IMS is primarily concerned with this level of improvement. Not all improvements will pay, and some will need to be filtered out, but creating a culture of improvement seeking is more important. Toyota estimates that the top 2.5% of ideas pay for their entire recognition program.

Level 2: The Work Team or Mini Kaizen
Teams that work in a cell or on a line segment undertake an improvement workshop affecting their collective work area. These activities may be done "on the fly" whenever they arise.

Level 3: Kaizen Blitz or Point Kaizen
The Blitz event is carried out in the local area but requiring larger resources and more time, usually a 3-5 day full time event. These address more complex issues than the group can handle on their own and are usually supported by others within the company. An example would be an emergency department layout change or a machine changeover reduction project. Remember, however, that a kaizen event is a "batch idea" process, so should not be the only, or even the major, forum for ideas and improvements.

Level 4: Value Stream Improvements: Flow Kaizen
Flow kaizen works across a full internal value stream, taking weeks to three months for a project. They are the prime engine for realising an identified Lean future state action plan. The value stream map identifies obstacles to flow in the system and thus kaizen events are targeted at these areas to remove each bottleneck sequentially and improve overall system flow.

Often, a Lean mapping project will result in an Implementation Plan comprising all the above levels. These activities are sometimes called "Do its" for levels 1 and 2, "Events" for level 3, and "Projects" for level 4. These are set out against a time line, or "Master Schedule" that aims to bring about the "Future State" in a specific period – typically 6 months.

Level 5: Supply Chain Kaizen
This is concerned with improving the end to end supply chain - many times, from raw material/information to the product/service being in the hands of the customer. This is similar in concept to level 4 but the focus is across many organisations.

Idea Management Models

There are two main types of IMS models, namely the centralised model, and the decentralised model (Kaizen Style).

The Centralised Model

All improvement suggestions from employees are submitted to the idea office managed by an idea manager. Usually the idea manager sends the evaluation and responsibility for implementation to a subject matter expert who has special expertise and cost responsibility for the idea.

Advantages of the Centralised Model
- standardised approach
- improves acceptance of breakthrough ideas

Disadvantages of the Centralised Model
- "red tape" slows down process
- creates ways to avoid local managers in the process
- fails to provide help for idea submitters through co-development of their ideas and the resultant up-skilling

The Decentralised Model

In the decentralised model, ideas are the responsibility of local work teams. Ideas for improvements are submitted to the direct supervisor. The supervisor can accept or decline the idea and allow the employee implementation ownership if the idea is feasible. Supervisors can help refine or enhance the idea, and if the idea is implemented the supervisor can provide recognition to the employee. Historically this is the best performing idea system model by some distance.

Advantages of the decentralised model
- reduced administration
- reduced turnaround time
- greater involvement by local manager/supervisor
- immediate recognition
- easier to generate team based ideas
- employee skills development

Disadvantages of the decentralised model
- inconsistency of approach between managers/supervisors
- greater training required

Other Models:
- Work based systems such as Quality Circles and Kaizen Blitz Teams
- Supervisory Model is where the supervisor does everything!
- Informal systems are where there are no formal methods for collecting ideas, idea generation and evaluation is passively left to normal line management processes.
- Open door policy where employees are free to drop in to their managers at any time to give feedback and ideas etc.

Two Related Aspects on Ideas:

Problem Solving & Improvement

The Lean Philosophy strives to make the process visible so that abnormal conditions and problems are revealed as soon as they occur. The systems design is supported so that these problems are counter-measured immediately and are stayed with until the root causes have been dissolved. Indeed problems are viewed as opportunities for improvement and for engaging the creative involvement of the people working the processes. Problems are opportunities because they identify gaps in our current knowledge. There are infinite problems and opportunities to improve in all processes; hence no problem is a problem!

> "No one has more trouble, than the person who claims to have no trouble."
> (Having no problems is the biggest problem of all.)
> Taiichi Ohno

What is an Idea?

One question that often arises is what defines an idea? This is a practical, relevant question for organisations on the lean journey as they seek to design their processes and systems to make problems immediately noticeable. Many people are involved in daily problem solving and the implementation of employees' creative ideas to countermeasure and dissolve root cause(s) of these problems. If an IMS is to gain traction it needs to be integrated and aligned with the existing methodology for problem solving. Employees must be encouraged to use the IMS as the well oiled mechanism for supporting them in the implementation of their ideas for problem resolution. Employees become skilled in problem solving by active participation and putting into practice their own ideas. Therefore ideas from problem solving should be included in the IMS; indeed it must strongly nurture problem solving.

Ideas may not be related to problem solving. Or can they? Lean views problems as opportunities, indeed gifts! Are not all observed gaps from True North idea targets? Chuck Yorke elegantly states that an idea is something YOU can act on. If you can't take action then it's just a wish or a dream. It is not just problem identification; the emphasis is on participation and implementation by the idea originator. An idea is something that provides a different way of doing something for a period, until the next cycle of continuous improvement provides a better known way.

Recently retired Toyota Vice President for Human Resources Pete Gritton, who now works as an Improvement Advisor to organisations, shared some insights on this. He stated that many ideas implemented through problem solving at Toyota are routed through the company's suggestion system. However not all of them are; it depends to a large extent on the originator's desire to put their problem solving ideas through the process. The practical reason for this is that some extra paperwork is required in terms of writing up the idea and putting it forward. Temporary countermeasures from problem solving are normally not considered for the suggestion system. It is when the complete PDSA cycle has been completed and countermeasures are verified as having solved the problem that the option is open to submit the ideas as a record.

The foundation of a good idea system is based on the realisation that there is far more capability/capacity in our people than is actually being harnessed. The essence of the

Lean Philosophy is developing within each employee an improvement seeking and waste elimination mindset.

We commonly hear; "That's already happening here, we just don't write the ideas down". However is there anything else that we do that is important to us like, for example your expense system that you don't have a process for? Ideas are too important to be left to chance and in the absence of a defined process they will be pushed to the back burner due to urgent day to day pressures.

If everyone even improved their job 0.1% everyday that adds up to almost a 25% improvement per employee year on year. That equates to a colossal competitive advantage over time and competitors cannot copy these compounded small improvements.

Employees are coached as to what constitutes a good idea. "Bad ideas" are viewed as training opportunities; the intent behind the idea is teased out and put forward again.

So again, a good idea system builds problem consciousness and is integrated into the daily work processes to support this non-stop incremental improvement. The mentors are encouraged to frame the problems to enable maximum learning and development of their staff. This engages employees through the excitement of seeing their own ideas being used to produce change that results in improvement. Consistent with Imai's Kaizen Flag concept prevoiusly, these ideas are the primary focus of the IMS.

There is no end to improvement opportunities if we become sensitized to waste as the thought provoking quote from Shigeo Shingo reveals.

"If the nut has fifteen threads on it, it cannot be tightened unless it is turned fifteen times. In reality, though, it is that last turn that tightens the bolt and the first one that loosens it. The remaining fourteen turns are waste."

Creativity and Innovation

The Kaizen Flag also points out that we need to make time available for creativity and innovation to help keep the organisation ahead of the pack. In Chapter 7 we explore this concept and how we can foster a culture of continuous creativity and innovation.

Chapter 3   Idea Management Systems

In this chapter we consider both "hard" tool and technique based aspects, and "soft" or people aspects of idea management. Of course, these two overlap.

Hard Aspects

We begin this section by looking at two effective methods to stimulate ideas. We then go on to consider the related issues of visual management and measurement.

Whilst everyone should be aware of opportunities for improvement, and feel confident in putting those ideas forward, almost everyone experiences a form of blindness to opportunity that results from daily, repetitive activity. Two examples (water carrying and toilet flush) were given in the opening section of the book. Ah! But they are always obvious after the fact. "Why did no-one think of that before?"

Many management concepts are initially successful simply because they offer new ways of looking at old problems. Some continue, some fade. Hence business process re-engineering, six sigma, operations research, and indeed Lean and idea management itself. The following two methods use this renewal theme.

Focus

Focus is about creating an awareness of a current issue that is important to the organisation or its customers. Examples include lead-time reduction, excess inventory, paperwork, e-mails, or specific problems like rust, packaging, or date-expired goods. A general theme or focus such as cost reduction is usually too wide, although a specific cost reduction focus on, say, travel or energy may well prove successful. Certainly, a focus on people reduction is not going to work!

A Focus or theme should not just be announced, but explained and supported by posters, screen savers, briefings, and of course by manager interest and involvement. The need should be made clear. A good way, entirely compatible with Lean, is via Policy Deployment that includes a roll-down, participative, "catchball" process using Plan Do Study Act and lasting for a specific period.

Idea focus has often yielded amazing results from previously "hidden" areas. At one local UK authority, a focus on reducing paperwork saved hundreds of unnecessary pages of printed reports and copies in the first month – resulting from a conversion to electronic means, avoiding "just in case" duplication, re-order quantities, paper sizes, and elimination by questioning the use made of various forms.

Idea Surfacing

Idea Surfacing, or "Enforced Problem solving" was mentioned in Chapter 1. Here, instead of a passive, "hoping for it to happen" approach, ideas are surfaced by numerous activities. In manufacturing, Toyota has been the master of this by methods such as the andon (or line-stop) chord, inventory withdrawal by taking out kanbans (one less than last time), 5S activities (for example to highlight missing tools on a shadow board), SPC charts, failsafe (pokayoke) devices, and various Lean tools such as value stream mapping. In service, awareness of concepts such as failure demand (demand that should not be there but is), "system conditions" (typically targets and measures that distort system performance – like a quota on calls per hour in a call centre), but also SPC and failsafing, help to highlight issues. An important idea in both service and manufacturing is the root-cause question. Thus, not just "solving" the present problem, but asking why it arose in the first place.

The Toyota system and Eli Goldratt's Theory of Constraints are both well known for their Socratic methodology. Never give "the answer", but question so that people discover for themselves.

Idea Surfacing requires active insistence that issues that are highlighted are followed up. This, of course, takes time and that is a major reason why it is not being done. But it's the old story about sharpening the axe – no time to sharpen because you are too busy chopping down the tree.

Some of the actual tools used in Problem Surfacing are described in more detail in Chapter 5.

Visual Management of Ideas

Visual management is integral to both of these methods. Keep the idea process in front of employees. Show the sources of ideas, show progress, show the results. People are less likely to voice constructive meaningful ideas to a suggestion box on the wall, but are far more likely to share ideas with a supervisor or manager who actively looks for and encourages ideas. The "secret" of course is for the supervisor to enquire. Software packages can be used in tandem to track and reduce review time and to automate metric generation, but the physical presence of the board at the workplace cannot be overstated.

The figure below details the elegant simplicity of the way ideas move through the process:
- First, ideas are submitted (**Idea**)
- Second, they are screened and either advanced to a queue or sent for enrichment/pending review (**To Do**)
- Third, they become actively worked on (**Doing**)
- Fourth, implementation is complete (**Done**)
(adapted from Mann 2005)

Idea	To Do	Doing	Done

Visual Idea Board

Section One

Financial Return on Investment

The power and philosophy of an IMS is captured in the quotation below:

"Why did we hire 55,000 employees and only use three of them? We never asked four magic words, "What do you think?" Woody Morcult, Former CEO of Dana (Bodek 2004).

The examples shown in this section detail the tangible financial returns from some of the leading practitioners worldwide.

Examples of dramatic financial returns are-:

1. Subaru 2003: 7,800 employees, $5246 per employee, they saved $40 million. The investment in training was $70 per employee or $546K in total. This represented a return on investment of 73:1 (Bodek 2005).

2. At the conclusion of American Airlines year-long "Brainwaves" program, they purchased a $50.3 million Boeing 757 called "Pride of America" with the money they saved (Robinson & Schroeder 2004). They have also purchased a Boeing 777 called "American Spirit, IdeAAs In Flight", worth $150 million from the savings on employee ideas. In the first 14 years of their IdeAAs system they have saved $593 million from employee ideas (Business Wire Jan 30 2001).

3. In February of 2001, Southwest Airlines' CEO Herb Kelleher sent a letter to every employee asking each worker to identify a way to save $5.00 a day. In six weeks, this large corporation found ways to save more than $2 million (Lengnick-Hall 2002).

4. Toyota gets 1.5 million ideas per year saving $300 million annually (Source: www.Leanaffiliates.com).

5. Matsushita (Panasonic), Isuzu, Sanyo and others claim to save more than $3,000 per year per employee. Imagine Panasonic claims more than $175 million was saved in 2002 from its employees' improvement ideas (Source: www.Leanaffiliates.com).

6. In ideasUK 2002-03 members saved the equivalent of $480 million (Source: ideasUK).

7. MasterCard saved $115 million in 18 months from its Priceless Ideas Program (Source: www.suggestionshemes.com).

These figures are impressive. But, beware! If the prime metric of an IMS is to generate impressive savings figures there may be a great temptation to cheat with the numbers. We don't believe that was the case here, but certainly many Six Sigma programs have become notorious in claiming savings that turn out to be wildly exaggerated. Bob Chapman, CEO of Barry-Wehmuller, and an inspirational Lean leader, says that simply asking staff about how they felt about CI initiatives is far better than collecting the numbers. If the program is right, the numbers will follow!

Documenting Ideas is Key
One of the hardest things to instil during implementation of an IMS is to ensure that *ALL* ideas are written down. It is vital that the reasons for this are communicated to participants.

- When ideas are written down you can see what has changed and where, and who is involved in stimulating this type of improvement. The objective is that ideas will be leveraged across different areas of the organisation. At a Dana plant in the US one idea was copied 56 times across the division within a few weeks of been shared (SME 2004 DVD II).

"Talent is always conscious of its own abundance and doesn't object to sharing"
Alexander Solzhenitsyn.

- It gives employees personal pride about being allowed to participate fully in the improvement process. People feel like important stakeholders in the organisation.

- When ideas are visible, you can stimulate and involve all the work teams by having them read the ideas and provide their own.

- You write it down to sustain the activity. It is the constant doing and sharing that stirs others to get involved. If only a fraction of the workforce are doing it, or only temporarily doing it, Kaizen will never become a normal part of the daily work.

- Ideas are forgotten and lost trying to keep up with the pace and fervour of the daily work demands.

- Sharing ideas often leads to another cycle of ideas by triggering and cross pollinating additional uses for the idea etc.

- By sharing ideas the originator has self-expressed accountability to their peers to implement the change.

- By sharing kaizen cards, people naturally recognise that everybody has opportunities to improve, indeed there is no end to improvement options.

Measurement and the Effectiveness of the IMS

(surprise...not merely $!)

If we are not keeping the score we are just practising. It is noteworthy that too few metrics are as bad as too many; metrics must cut through to the vital key success factors for maintaining the system. However, it is not just the metric – it is the culture in which the metric is used that is crucial. Is the metric for reward and punishment, focused upwards on reporting, or is it there to uncover opportunities, focused downwards on improvement? As Deming said, 'Drive out Fear' is the pre-requisite. A very small number of metrics are needed to monitor and improve an Idea Management System. Such metrics should be aligned with the organisation strategy and goals. The table below gives an indication of areas for idea management.

Measurement	How it is Measured	Best In Class
Participation	The number of people who have submitted an idea over a certain time period. A person is only counted once, regardless of the number of ideas submitted. Some organisations base participation on implemented ideas instead of submitted ideas.	> 80%
Ideas/Employee	Total number of ideas completed for the time period divided by the total number of employees at the end of that time period.	> 24/Yr
Savings/ Employee	Total savings for the time period divided by the total number of eligible employees at the end of that time period. Savings normally should be net which is gross savings minus implementation, recognition, & administration costs.	> $3,000/Yr
Adoption Rate	The percentage of ideas that have been adopted in relation to all ideas that have had a decision made (adopt or not adopt)	> 80%
Average Total Turn-Around Time	The total time of processing the idea from submittal to final processing. For a not adopted idea that typically is when that decision was made. For an implemented idea it is when the idea is implemented and all paperwork is finished.	< 7 Days
Average Decision (Evaluation) Turn-Around Time	The average time taken to review an idea as viable (adopt or not adopt decision).	24~72 hours

Common Metrics (Source: adapted from Japan HR Association)

Soft Aspects

Rewards and Recognition

Give a percentage of overall savings as a reward for the idea? Don't go there!! With monetary rewards there are winners and losers: to overcome this you should make ideas and creativity part of the job. The prospect of reward (cash) encourages people to take the quickest and surest (not necessarily the most creative) route towards gaining it. In other words the goal becomes the reward and the reward itself captures much of their interest and energy. In the race for the reward, not only is creativity sacrificed, but opportunities for what cognitive psychologists call incidental learning, the important knowledge and insight gained from such exploration are greatly reduced (adapted from Robinson & Schroeder 2004). Rewards are one of the major reasons for IMS failures. Communicate the reasons why monetary rewards are not employed. Idea practitioners are not motivated by money or power but by intellectual stimulation and the excitement of seeing ideas transformed into reality (Davenport, T; Prusak, L; & Wilson, J 2003).

The differences between reward and recognition are detailed below. According to Alfie Kohn, in *Punished by Rewards*, only intrinsic rewards motivate over the medium and long term. Extrinsic rewards fade fast, become expected, and may often lead to destructive behaviour. Intrinsic motivation is the natural desire that people have to do a good job and make a positive difference. It is the spiritual reward a person gets from making an improvement to their work (Robinson & Stern 2004). Intrinsic motivation is increased when people feel that they can have some impact on the work that they perform. Intrinsic motivation is the difference between saying "you couldn't pay me enough to do that", and "I can't believe I'm getting paid to do this!" A system designed for rapid implementation of ideas cultivates this intrinsic motivation, in some cases to the point where money can be eliminated from the picture altogether (Robinson & Schroeder 1998).

Extrinsic motivation is work done in expectation of (typically) a monetary reward. This can be extremely harmful to an IMS as the process to implement the idea can be driven entirely by the anticipation of the reward and hence open to dysfunctional behaviours such as cheating, withholding information, and discouraging teamwork.

Let us distinguish between "rewards" and "recognition":

- A reward is something offered as compensation for an achievement. The message implied is that the person went above and beyond the call of normal duty. Examples include cash and stock options.

- Recognition is to show appreciation for resourcefulness in making a positive impact. The message implied is that the person is a valued member of the organisation and that their self initiated efforts are both valued and seen to have a positive influence. Examples include praise, celebration, and a personal "thank you".

Cash has low lasting impact value, indeed research studies have concluded that non cash recognition delivers a 6:1 ROI over direct cash awards. The recognition has to be something that the employees want – which is different in various areas of the world and also locally within the same work team! Lunch with the boss may be one person's worst nightmare, another's ultimate experience. For some, plaques belong on the mantelpiece. Others would rather use them as firewood! Involving the recogniser and those involved in the design, implementation and measurement of the recognition process is a necessary first step. If the answer to the "what do you want" question is money, the follow-up question "what would you use it for" may provide the true motivator (adapted from Schwarz 2008).

We are unable to harness the power of the people because of our propensity to suppress the frontline worker. Paying people for ideas blocks kaizen and neutralises the power of people. Payment for ideas defeats the purpose. The situation brings to mind a favourite parable:

"An old woman lived alone on a street where boys played noisily every afternoon. One day the noise became too much and she called the boys into her house. She told them that she liked to listen to them play, but her hearing was failing and she could no longer hear their games. She asked them to come along each day and play noisily in front of her house. If they did, she would give them each a quarter. The youngsters raced back the following day, and they made a tremendous racket playing happily in front of the house. The old woman paid and asked them to return the following day. Again they played and made noise, and again she paid them for it. But this time she gave each boy only 20 cents, explaining that she was running out of money. On the following day, they got only 15 cents each. Furthermore, the old woman told them that she would have to reduce the

Section One

fee to a nickel on the fourth day. The boys then became angry and said they would not be back. It was not worth the effort, they said, to play for only a nickel a day"

(May 2007).

Most rewards are for taking the first step in the creative process which is often the easiest…what about ALL the people who participated in fulfilling the idea?

Idea Stages:

1. Someone comes up with an idea and puts it forward.
2. It may require some work to make it feasible. A team leader may assist.
3. The idea is championed to management and those affected by it.
4. The idea may need further development, refinement, and pilot-testing.
5. The idea may also need formal approval from appropriate authorities.
6. The idea has to be implemented.
7. The actual effect of the idea has to be assessed.
8. Customer's, suppliers and employees have to be helped to "buy in" to the change.
9. The idea should be shared and spread throughout the company.
10. The idea needs to sustained - gain held by standard work or Poke Yoke etc (Adapted from Robinson & Schroeder 2004).

People required for tasks 2 to 10 often resent doing them if only the person doing task 1 (coming up with the idea and submitting it) gets rewarded. This results in stifled teamwork and usually bottlenecks in the process. Rewards substantially increase the cost, time, and effort needed to evaluate and implement ideas. The best systems rely on recognition and non monetary items.

Recognition Considerations

- The types of recognition that will be provided
- Method of calculating savings (if indeed considered necessary!)
- Individual, group and team recognition
- Type of recognition (best personalised to individual's tastes)
- Time period when the recognition will be bestowed or all through (at idea approval, implementation, after one year, etc)
- Centralised or decentralised local department budgets
- Do we recognise idea system evaluators, champions, etc

Recognition Examples:
- Quarterly award for the highest number of ideas
- Newsletter announcement for all winners
- Participation in the company's annual convention with a chance to win a host of prizes

- Monthly raffles for idea participants
- Attendance at conference and training courses
- Creativity reward for some rejected ideas
- Polo shirts for prolific idea participants
- Praise – a personal "thank you" can mean a lot
- Publicity of the people associated with the idea – photo in company newsletter etc.
- Feedback – peer recognition
- Cinema tickets – promotes family involvement
- Gift vouchers or "Idea Dollars"– employee can pick from catalogue items that have special meaning to them
- Merchandise – example is milestone points where the person can exchange these for items when they have accumulated predefined points from multiple implemented ideas

Recognition takes little or no money; the most important components of it are expediency and genuineness. We are all motivated by different things; hence the best policy is for the supervisors and team leaders to know what motivates each individual on their team. Then use a variety of recognition methods tailored to enhance each individual's motivation to participate.

As long as the intended recognition has meaning to people it can cause them to do extraordinary things. Think what people will go through to win coveted sporting medals. How can you create that nostalgic value for your company's recognition symbols?

The most powerful incentive to hand in an idea is the confidence that it will be given a fair hearing and will be implemented if it is recognised as a sound one. The optimal recognition system that a company can set up is a process that ensures ideas are handled quickly and effectively. Indeed there is no better recognition in seeing your idea in use and helping the daily work activities.

Human Potential

"Man's mind, once stretched to a new idea, never regains its original dimensions" Oliver Wendell Holmes Jr.

Many organisations see only workers hands, but the Lean mindset sees their brains. People are the only asset that appreciates over time; every other asset depreciates! Your company's skills stockpile is the type of inventory you don't want to reduce in your Lean transformation. Every time you hire a new pair of hands it comes with a complementary brain. A major reason why people don't like work is that they can't use their creative and problem solving skills. If you ask what's good for the people, paradoxically the company will benefit.

"Treat people as though they were what they ought to be, and you will help them become what they are capable of being." Goethe

Culture

The idea process leads to a positive, high performance culture. As employees see their ideas implemented, they begin to feel a more valued part of the team. They feel respected. This all leads to increasingly better ideas. Managers gain greater respect for their employees, as they see the quantity and quality of their ideas surface. Employees are trusted with more information, training, and authority. A true win-win scenario develops.

> *"Ironically, the projects that begin small and with cultural goals often generate greater proportional financial returns than those with economic goals"*
> *(Kanter 1997)*

The lesson is that if you focus on developing the people and giving them a chance to grow and learn; their changed attitudes will deliver the financial results for the organisation.

Motivation/Morale

A Gallup Organisation Study stated that only 28% of US workers are actively engaged at work. The majority 54% are just putting in their time. Although they have reasonable productivity, they are not putting their energy or passion into the job. And worse again 17% are actively disengaged. It is estimated that this group alone cost the US economy $350 billion a year (Buckingham 2002). Hence the potential power of employee involvement via implementing their ideas. When workers are not striving to change and improve their methods they often become bored with their work. The time goes a lot more rapidly when you are involved and looking for ways to improve.

Maslow's hierarchy of needs ranges from basic needs such as survival to the top level need of self actualisation. It is only when the lower levels are fully or partially satisfied that we look to have a higher level need satisfied. The left hand side of the table below lists Maslow's needs and on the right hand side is what an idea program can contribute.

Level 5: Self Actualisation Needs	Employees develop and learn new skills coordinating the implementation of their ideas
Level 4: Esteem Needs	Employees experience a "spiritual" reward seeing their idea implemented, used and recognised
Level 3: Social Needs	People interact implementing ideas and are involved in the decision making process
Level 2: Security & Safety Needs	Empowered employees can control their immediate work area
Level 1: Basis Physiological Needs (survival)	Implemented improvement ideas help the company survive

Maslow's "Hierarchy of Needs" Motivation Table

An IMS should energise the workforce. It's not just the improvement ideas themselves but also the improvement in people's attitude and their engagement.

Closing Thoughts

Establishment of a successful IMS is a broad undertaking and there are a number of factors to be addressed. The sequence of implementation steps is detailed in chapter 4.

The primary focus of the kaizen style idea management is on small ideas from frontline employees' local areas where they can positively effect change with the cooperation of their supervisors. In order for this to be successful associates need a support plan of resources (both people and knowledge) and this is developed in the next chapter.

The IMS and the vision must reach everyone and be actively supported by all levels of management. Management cannot be just behind this in support, they need to be actively out in front driving it. Everyone in the organisation must know the system and have ready access to it.

The IMS must be easy to use. Simplicity is at the end of the process of refinement and should be the design intention. Few employees will participate in a system that is difficult to use.

The IMS must have strong follow through. Few people will send in ideas to a system that does not give them serious attention. At American Airlines, any idea that has not been fully processed within 150 days heads for the CEO's desk.

The IMS must document ideas. Getting people to share their ideas with others also fosters continuous learning and community building.

The IMS should be based on intrinsic motivation and skills development.
Initiatives focused on current specific business issues are most likely to result in implemented ideas. More effective IMS's encourage its use as part of daily work. Integrate idea implementation in all employees' personal performance plans and salary ranking. If you don't ask, you don't get. Simple, but how often is this true!

Chapter 4

IMS for Problem Solving and Improvement

Idea Management Implementation Roadmap
The purpose of this chapter is to provide an overview of the activities required to establish an IMS in your organisation. Both the cultural and technical sides need to be addressed to realise the potential performance improvement from an IMS.

IMS Cultural Integration
You must harness the power of human nature by engaging all staff at the outset to ensure that the IMS will be embedded into the fabric of the daily work culture.

Mobilise the Idea Management Office
This office becomes the driving force behind the system. It is made up of influential enthusiasts from all levels of the value stream including both senior/middle management and admired front-line staff. The group should also have learned the support skills discussed in the next chapter well enough to teach them.

Establish the Business Necessity for Ideas
Harvesting and implementing employee ideas should not just be a "nice" thing to do! The failure to create tension is a key mistake made by leaders when implementing new techniques. Need must drive change. Hence communication of why an IMS is needed should be delivered to engage management, unions (if applicable) and frontline staff. Emphasise the necessity to have everybody contributing to the success of the organisation through continually implementing small ideas that make the organisation stronger every day. Many organisations have barely scratched the surface in terms of optimising their on-site processes. It is common to see such processes off-shored to lower wage locations. There is perhaps more leverage to be gained by removal of waste from these on-site processes rather than outsourcing sub-optimised processes to lower wage locations. Our front-line employees as the experts are the best people to do this via persistent execution of small improvement ideas.

Create a Mission (or Purpose) and Vision and define Values and Goals

Mission - This is the concise description of what the IMS should deliver.

An example Mission Statement is:

"To cultivate the unseen potential of all our employees through the realisation of their improvement ideas."

Purpose - What the system is there to do. Sounds obvious? Maybe, but sub-systems are often blinded to the overall end-to-end purpose. Is the purpose to meet targets or to help customers? (These are not always the same thing! "Tell me how you will measure me, and I'll tell you what I will do".)

Vision - This is a clear and compelling picture of the future. Strive to make people believe (a sense of certainty) that a future in which everybody contributes and self-implements small ideas on a continual basis will be a better one.

An example Vision Statement is written below:

"All employees are empowered and supported to actively implement their ideas."

Values - Behaviours that we are striving to build and reinforce to ensure a continual stream of improvement ideas on a daily basis.

For example:

- Respect for individuals (trust that people know better methods and will do the right thing for the organisation)
- Encouragement of constructive dissatisfaction (continually seeking a better way)
- Low levels of fear existing throughout the organisation
- Failure viewed as experiments and a learning process
- Innovators who are encouraged and recognised
- Humour (changes our mental perspectives and jump starts our brain), ha ha leads to aha!

Far and away the biggest mistake managers make is ignoring the crucial importance of alignment (Collins 2004). Allow frontline employees to participate in the crafting of your mission and vision statements, this fosters alignment and buy-in.

Goals - The objectives of the IMS to be communicated in order of priority are:

- Improving and developing people's skills through self-implementation of their ideas with guidance from subject matter experts where necessary
- **All** employees evolve into dual roles of doing the work **and** being proactive in process improvement using their thinking skills. This involvement leads to increased employee morale and higher feelings of accomplishment.
- Improved processes leading to enhanced customer satisfaction and company performance

Engage Employees at All Levels & Communicate the Vision

Ensure that senior management is supportive and understands the power of a well designed and run IMS. Show data from leading companies of dramatic financial and employee engagement results and also of the enormous multiplier effects from leveraged small ideas. The timeless wisdom that looking after the means (employees) ensures that the ends (financial returns) will take care of themselves is especially pertinent here.

Release the potential of your employees and your employees will release the potential of your organisation (Barlow, S., Parry, S. & Faulkner, M. 2005). That is, ultimately, the front line produces the bottom line.

The most difficult part of starting up an effective system is persuading management to dedicate adequate resources to survive the start up. The initial flood of ideas is due to the release of all the ideas that people had over time, but had no practical outlet to realise them (Robinson & Stern 1998).

IMS expectations need to be communicated to the frontlines via employees' personal performance plans, start-up meetings, team information boards etc. Understanding these expectations, being able to teach and inspect for them and holding supervisors accountable for implementing them personally at an appropriate pace is key. Use a communication plan to help with this vital aspect.

The following is a sample of some activities to enable smooth integration:

- Creativity is actively encouraged by frontline supervisors
- Managers are compensated and rated on the basis of the number of ideas implemented by their teams
- Ideas per employee are a key measure for associate annual performance reviews
- Ideas are fast tracked into realisation by a robust system
- Regular creativity workshops are held to boost idea implementation and are kicked off by senior management
- Time is allocated within the job function of all employees to work on ideas: Lean concept of under-capacity scheduling is a natural way to integrate idea activity as a normal part of daily work. Technical and maintenance functions typically assume a heavy workload from the IMS and management must ensure that resources be allocated for this crucial function
- People are recognised for supporting the process
- Open communication channels allow access to information and resources that are required for idea implementation

Idea Management Principles & Systems Training

Can you train for ideas? A requirement is to set free the latent potential dormant in an organisation's people. As the saying goes "men would rather die than think". The purpose of the training is to motivate people to use their potential and to provide tools and techniques to break long established habits and ways of viewing the world.

Employees should be brought through an overview presentation covering why ideas are needed and the power of creating an idea friendly culture. Training modules must be developed on the various characteristics of the IMS and delivered. Also consideration needs to be given to how Lean and the principles and tools can be harnessed to maximise the raising of ideas.

From the "Passive" viewpoint (as discussed in Chapter 1), employees need to know why ideas are so important both for themselves and for the future prosperity and survival of the organisation. Of course, this must be more than words. Action on the part of management is needed, every day.

From the "Enforced" viewpoint, the use of every Lean tool is an opportunity to surface a problem. "If there is 'no problem' – that is the problem". A classic example of Lean problem surfacing is Toyota's Andon Line Stop System. Every time the cord is pulled there is an opportunity to surface a problem and to put forward a hypothesis towards its removal. And, at a typical Toyota plant, the chord is pulled 1200 times per day! If it is not pulled, this would indicate perfection – an impossible state. Note this is absolutely in accordance with Deming's "94/6" rule – that 94% of problems are due to the process, and only 6% due to the people. So, start with the process. Management needs to know about problems with the process as a pre-requisite to improving the process. And, management cannot possibly know about all the things that can go wrong. So management REQUIRES associates to surface and report problems, and not to "solve" or "work around" the same old problems every day.

The people driving the IMS need to know, and to be able to communicate a few key principles. They are:

Communication Plan

An often neglected aspect is good communication. If you are serious about creating an idea receptive culture, you must pay attention to communication before, during, and after launch. Experts recommend, as rule of thumb, to do five times the communication that you feel is adequate!

TO WHOM	WHAT	WHEN
All Staff – Tailor to specific expectations to enable success e.g. Management emphasise the financial returns Employees emphasise the engagement and up-skilling benefits	- IMS Overview – What and Why? - System Infrastructure - Support Requirements - etc	- Prior to launch and throughout system lifecycle

Example of a partial Communication Plan

Develop "Learn - Apply - Reflect" Training

Ideally the tools should be taught to associates on a pull basis as demanded by the idea at hand, then they should be experimented with to dissolve the problem or realise the opportunity. Finally the associate should endeavour to complete the learning cycle for each idea investigation with an After Action Review with their supervisor to reinforce insights acquired by answering the following questions:
- What did we set out to do?
- What did we actually do?
- What have we learned?
- What are we going to do?

The key to an effective training program is to explain the purpose of employee involvement (Imberman 1986) – that is improving people's capabilities via them personally implementing improvement ideas.

"I cannot teach anyone anything; I can only make them think".

Socrates

It is important that leadership understands why ideas are important. Many are surprised at the potential for performance improvement that lies in employee ideas (Robinson & Schroeder 2004).

Section Two

Training Topics for Consideration

Develop and deliver training packages from the material covered in this book tailored to each stakeholders needs to address the following:
- The *What* and the *Why* of Idea Management
- Key Driving Forces to enhance
- Restraining Forces to diminish
- Structure for idea capture, realisation, and sustaining
- Guiding people in writing ideas
- Alert to opportunities and problem surfacing
- Lean Overview and its requirement for a continual idea stream
- Creative Thinking skills
- Practical examples
- Problem solving
- Reward & Recognition
- Roles
- Evaluation
- Promotion/Campaigns
- Ballpark cost saving calculations from tangible ideas
- Conflict Resolution

Roles and Responsibilities to Support the IMS

Perhaps the biggest challenge to establishing a successful IMS is that there is a sizeable requirement in terms of time to support idea implementation. Or so it would appear. But "fixing" a problem every day is hugely wasteful when compared with a root cause solution taking some time but only being done once. Hence, the seemingly wasteful practice of providing extra capacity to allow proper kaizen. Stephen Covey talks about four quadrants in relation to effective use of our time and making time available for proactive work. The four are:

1. Important - Urgent: such as fire-fighting
2. Not Important - Urgent: such as interruptions, many meetings
3. Not Important - Not Urgent: such as time stealers
4. Important - Not Urgent: such as proactive improvement ideas

The last quadrant often seems a nice to do, however this is where we need to spend more time in as this is the important work that assures the organisation's future. Hence this requires that we stop doing or guard against having our day absorbed by quadrants 2 and 3 especially. Conscious awareness of this matrix can help ensure that we allow time for everyday improvement ideas.

Roles need to be created or modified to embed the IMS into the work culture. These include:

Idea Coach

This role is typically an internal IMS expert. Their primary responsibility includes designing and setting up the IMS infrastructure in various areas of the organisation and supporting it until they are self sustaining. This role can often be a full time position in larger organisations and this person can develop and deliver some of the training modules. They would mentor and coordinate the activities of the local idea management offices described below. This person however is not the day to day driver. An IMS needs to be championed and owned at the local level and must not be seen as "their" program. The Idea Coach is the "go to" person for any road blocks that can arise in the various decentralised IMS's across the organisation. This role is particularly effective in building bridges between management and the frontlines. The coach needs to ensure that ideas align with the current business needs.

Local Idea Management Steering Group

The role of the Idea Management Steering Group is to develop the strategies and guidelines for the IMS. The office identifies and highlights roadblocks to senior management to ensure seamless integration into the daily activities. The Idea Coach would be a member. Other members would include senior managers from all major functions. Membership should rotate.

The Office is responsible for the development and support of the following critical areas of success: measurement, training, recognition, communication, targeted campaigns for specific idea themes such as safety etc, marketing, software support (if required) and the ongoing development of the idea management process. They should meet weekly to review the system performance, resolve issues and continuously keep it fresh and invigorated.

Senior & Middle Management

Employees will only have confidence in the IMS and use it, if it is actively supported and encouraged by senior/middle management. The leadership MUST BELIEVE in the creative potential and untapped power of its frontline employees and actively support them. Without this the idea system will surely never reach its potential and probably fail. Many successful IMS's have a "champion" at senior level who is committed to it and willing to promote it within the organisation and eliminate roadblocks. This commitment must be visible and continuous.

In Yasuda's book "40 Years, 20 Million Ideas" he pointed out that ever since 1951, a top executive has headed Toyota's Idea Management System. This executive has included several future CEO's and chairmen, and even members of the founding Toyoda family.

Supervisors and Team Leaders

Supervisors and team leaders play a vital role in the idea process. They make sure the necessary resources are available to evaluate, filter, test, and implement the ideas. Their role is to continually encourage and challenge. A front line operator may not have the time to develop ideas fully, so needs the help of first and second tier management. They also must have facilitation skills to conduct small group improvement activities or local Kaizen. Of course, time for these activities must be built into their activities. In the Training Within Industry (TWI) approach, a supervisor has five responsibilities – meeting the schedule, job instruction (including job breakdown analysis, standard work, and teaching new employees), job methods (including improvement), job relations (working with the team), and job safety. The supervisor acts as the gatekeeper of employee ideas and is the channel that transforms the traditional suggestion scheme into a modern best practice idea management process. Of course, team leaders and supervisors must act quickly to help implement ideas, or at the very least give rapid feedback as to why an idea cannot be implemented, either not at all or not immediately.

With the decentralised model the local supervisor handles the ideas from employees. Normally they discuss and filter the ideas with their employees and if required help them enrich the ideas and develop them further. The supervisor can decide about implementation and recognition.

Local Idea Champion

In some cases, where there is no team leader, each local work team should have an Idea Champion (preferably a front line associate) who performs the following activities:
- Promotes ideas in their area

- Provides training and information

- Maintenance and distribution of metrics

- Connects with managers needs and aligns ideas with current issues

- Engages technical and support staff

- Takes part in daily Gemba Walks and daily idea board readings

Frontline Associate

Employees are expected bring problems to the attention of team leaders and supervisors (that is, to surface problems) and to come up with ideas relating to their solution. The first priority is ideas that they can implement themselves. The second priority is ideas that relate to the work of others. Generally, it is not acceptable to always come up with ideas for others to do. Idea generation is part of their normal work. But the collection and development of ideas must be made as easy as possible, and this is where team leaders and supervisors have a vital role.

Idea Standard Work

The very phrase "standard work" may appear to some to be in direct conflict with Idea Management. Not so. Ideas need to be fostered in a standard system that leads ideas to flow from source to implementation. Jeffrey Liker refers to the "Toyota Paradox" whereby standards are the very thing that ensures development and creativity. Like "rules of engagement" in the military that empower soldiers to take action in a whole range of circumstances. A good standard actually absorbs variety, rather than restricts it.

Idea standard work is a series of activities developed by consensus that must be carried out daily to support the IMS. For example, ensuring that visual controls are maintained, and time is allotted to implement ideas at specified times each shift. Following idea standard work (see below table) ensures that the principal elements of the IMS are maintained so as to unleash its potential.

Who	What	Why	When
Idea Management Office	• Design & maintain the IMS • Promote the IMS • Monitor Metrics • Hold review meetings • Organise benchmarking and conference attendances • Lead recognition events • Co-ordinate larger "Project" ideas • Audit and continually improve the IMS • Be accountable for IMS growth • Join local Employee Involvement Association • Attend "Idea Board" readings • Spread ideas internally and with sister organisations	• To include everyone in C.I • Integration into daily culture • To monitor performance and sustain • To review ideas • To stimulate interest and C.I • To encourage participation • To ensure that all ideas are addressed • Grow the IMS and prevent slippage • Harvest the latent potential of people • External Best Practice expertise • Shows support and ideas are valued • Leverage the potential of good solutions	• Continuous • Continuous • Weekly • Weekly • Quarterly • Weekly • Monthly • Every 6 months • Continuous • Yearly • Daily • Weekly Con. Call
Senior Management	• Visibly support the process • Ensure adequate budget • Attend for recognition events • Remove roadblocks • Review idea activity as part of all employee's performance reviews • Review metrics at site meetings • Attend "Idea Board" readings • Implement or co-ordinate implementation of two ideas/month	• Show that ideas are part of the job • Supports the process and recognition • Shows that ideas are valued • Ensure smooth running of the system • Career advancement is linked to IMS • What gets measured gets done! • Recognition and sustaining activity • Lead by example by participating	• Continually • Quarterly • Monthly • As required • Every 6 months • Weekly • Daily • Minimum of 2 ideas/month
Middle Management	• Visibly support the process • Provide expertise to ideas as needed • Mentor frontlines during implementation • Verbally ask for ideas during waste walks • Teach problem solving and creativity tools • Facilitate idea workshops • Promote the IMS • Implement or co-ordinate implementation of two ideas/month	• Show support • See idea through to completion • Up-skill the frontline employees • Keep organization competitive • Up-skill associates and site capability • Give the system a boost • Help release latent talent of people • Lead by example by participating	• Continually • As pulled by ideas • As pulled by ideas • Daily • As pulled by ideas • Monthly • Continually • Minimum of 2 ideas/month

Maintenance & I.T. Support	• Visibly support the process • Mentor frontlines during implementation • Implement ideas that are solely suited to their skill-set • Verbally ask for ideas • Provide reps for waste walks • Implement or co-ordinate implementation of two ideas/month	• Show support • Up-skill associates • See idea through to completion • Maintain competitiveness • Provide technical resource • Lead by example by participating	• Continually • As pulled by ideas • As pulled by ideas • Daily • Daily • Minimum of 2 ideas/month
Supervisors	• Visibly support the process • Appoint resources to implement larger ideas • Champion the recognition process • Report IMS metrics • Mentor associates on filtering ideas & during implementation • Verbally ask for ideas • Teach problem solving & creativity tools • Facilitate idea workshops • Promote the IMS • Audit the "Idea Board" & "Hall of Fame" • Provide associates on the frontlines with feedback • Attend waste walks • Knowledge of what motivates each member of their team • Provide conflict resolution facilitation • Implement or co-ordinate implementation of two ideas/month	• Integrate into normal work • See idea through to completion • Keep the IMS invigorated • Measure performance • Up-skill associates on the frontlines • Human interaction is the best method • Everyone knows how to solve problems • Give the IMS a boost • Help release the latent talents of people • Recognition to participants and sharing • Transparency and shows idea is valued • Use aggregate knowledge to dissolve • Make recognition personally meaningful • Improvement means change • Lead by example by participating	• Daily meetings • As pulled by ideas • Continually • Weekly • As pulled by ideas • Daily • As pulled by ideas • Monthly • Continually • End of every shift • With 24/72 hours • Daily • Keep up to date • As required • Minimum of 2 ideas/month
Frontline Idea Champions	• Lead "Idea Board" Readings • Attend Waste Walks • Pull together raw data for metric reporting • Facilitate local workshops for idea generation sessions • Promote the IMS • Be the intermediary between the frontlines and management • Ask for, filter and monitor ideas • Electronically log implemented ideas • Implement or co-ordinate implementation of two ideas/month	• Build bridge with management & staff • Raise concerns at the frontlines • Monitor performance & C.I • Give the IMS a boost • Help release the latent talents of people • Improve relationships & teamwork • Alignment & Integration into daily work • Establish a knowledge portal • Lead by example by participating	• Continually • Daily • Weekly • Monthly • Every shift • Daily • Daily • Weekly • Minimum of 2 ideas/month

Frontline Employees	• Implement or co-ordinate implementation of two ideas/month • Representative at daily waste walks • Attend promotion & peer recognition events • Look for opportunities to copy and/or spread ideas	• Develop new skills and involvement • Frontlines know the problems best • Make it meaningful to recipient • Leveragability can be an immense opportunity	• Minimum of 2 ideas/month • Daily • Monthly • Quarterly

Idea Standard Work

Technical Implementation Guidelines

In parallel with the "soft" cultural buy-in summarised previously, the "hard" technical steps are also developed by the Idea Management Office members. There is no "one size fits all" solution, you have to "cut the cloth to suit the table", and proceed in a manner that suits your organisational culture. The steps outlined below are recommendations to help the team navigate the course for implementing an IMS into their organisation.

Milestone	Actions	Approx. Timeline
Enlist IMS Internal/External consultant support	• Use their expertise for system design and implementation and knowledge of benchmarking opportunities	Month One
Form and Idea Management Office	• Establish cross functional team from all levels of the value stream and determine meeting frequency	Month One
Utilise Change Management Techniques For Cultural Buy-in	• Establish the need for the IMS • Benchmark other successful IMS implementation(s) • Develop the mission, vision, desired values and objectives • Establish Management Support • Develop Communication Roll-Out Plan and commence delivery	Month One
Develop Idea Management Support Plan	• Teach IMS Theory and Support Plan to Idea Management Office Team Develop frontline "Idea Coaches" and "Idea Champions" • Develop shop floor "Gemba Walk" schedule • Develop Kaizen Booklets and Kaizen Cards • Develop Basic Problem Solving Tools and Lean Tools Instruction Packs • Develop Basic Creativity Tools Instruction Packs • Develop and strengthen Standardization (include. Standard Work, Visual Management & "Target Vs. Actual" Accountability) • Deliver tailored IMS Overview to Value Stream Senior Management • Deliver tailored IMS Overview to Supervisors • Deliver tailored IMS Overview to Engineering & Maintenance • Deliver tailored IMS Overview (include costing calculation methods) to frontline staff (detailed creativity and problem solving tools to be taught on a just-in-time basis as pulled by each individual's idea demands) • Show IMS training DVD's to all staff • Develop and agree Employee Task Standard Work with all Stakeholders • Teach idea sustaining tools to frontline staff such	Month Two

	as PDSA, TWI, and Standard Work • Gain buy-in and add new roles & responsibilities as defined in the Employee Idea Standard Work • Join local Employee Involvement Association	
Design	• Decide on the type of system (De-centralised in this case) • Design Idea Process Flow and Structure (include evaluation decision matrix and reporting metrics) • Involve HR and Legal (IP etc)	Month One
Administration	• Define and agree tasks with frontline supervisor • Design and Install "Idea Board" at the Gemba	Month Two
Assign "floating" Budget	• Agree budget with scope for flexibility depending on idea volume	Month Two
Promotion	• Develop Promotion Strategy	Month Two
Recognition	• Form Focus Groups with all stakeholders & gain consensus on employee recognition	Month Two
Rules	• Determine IMS Rules (simplicity is the end of the process of refinement!)	Month Three
Pilot Launch	• Launch workshop and pilot in small area • Prove success and spread across VSM	Month Three
Audit	• Audit the IMS after 6 months. Grade the status of the IMS, Platinum, Gold, Silver, or Bronze (see appendix II).	Month Six

Top Level IMS Implementation Plan

IMS Research

The implementation team researches IMS principles and theory (see chapter 2). The key people must learn the problem solving and creativity tools and cascade them throughout the targeted area where the IMS is being established.

Purchase books and DVD's on IMS's for training and education of employees. Join local employee involvement or ideas associations such as ideasUK or EIA (Employee Involvement Association of USA). They are a great help especially at the start-up phase.

The best IMS's are so completely ingrained into the way the organisation operates daily that they are indistinguishable from the other systems and processes (Robinson & Stern 98). Align other initiatives with the system to enable it to be successful and to avoid competing initiatives.

IMS Design

Identify the idea process flow and scope out the types of ideas targeted and who is eligible (ideally all employees). This chapter focuses on the decentralised model, meaning that the system is locally contained at the frontline team level. The focus is for ideas that are either self-implemented or implementation is overseen by the idea originator. Larger ideas are encouraged too but, are routed to a separate project type hopper (see process flow chart below). One consideration to keep in mind as the IMS grows and is leveraged into other value streams is to ensure that each decentralised IMS has links to every other, this could be coordinated by the site "Idea Manager or Coach". The purpose of this is to ensure consistency and maximum sharing and spread of ideas.

Idea Process Flow

- Inspire all employees to come up with two improvement ideas per month to make their work easier or more interesting, reduce costs, improve quality, improve the throughput, improve safety, improve customer service or to enhance patient care etc.

- Encourage employees to write down ideas on a Kaizen Card every time they find a problem, make a slip-up, or see an opportunity for improvement and post them on the "Idea" column of the Idea Board (see graphic of idea board in chapter 3). Whenever possible take or draw pictures of the before and after situations. Viewing a picture is easier than words and establishes clarity. A picture quickly explains the improvement idea and stimulates other people to do the same thing. We want people to copy each other to further the continuous improvement and get everyone involved. Copying stimulates even more and greater ideas.

- The idea generator evaluates and filters their idea with their peers (this saves supervisor evaluation time and improves the quality of ideas) to ensure it is suitable. The supervisor then responds to the originator normally within 24 hours (max 72 hours) of the idea been brought forward. A quick decision matrix is shown below. The rational is:

    (a) **Low Effort – Low Benefit** - Go for it! System is focused on small self-implemented ideas. It's employee participation in thinking about improvement ideas and the compounding return and ripple effect of thousands of these that adds up over time.

    (b) **Low Effort – High Benefit** - Go for it! An added bonus!

    (c) **High Effort – High Benefit -** Maybe. What is the return on investment and near term priorities?

    (d) **High Effort – Low Benefit -** Forget it. Not feasible. The exceptions would be if it were a safety concern or regulation issue.

    The supervisor should mentor and teach people who submit weak ideas so that they are able to submit better ones next time. Always remember that if you reject the idea the person feels rejected! Strive to enrich the ideas with the originator and if this is not possible be tactful and explain the reasons why it's not feasible at this time. Also be welcoming of issues and problems that are brought forward, even if they are not accompanied with a solution yet, these are also great potential opportunities.

    Consider the ripple (spread) effect for all ideas and the impact that these may have across the entire organisation.

	High		
High	Go for it!	Maybe	
Benefit			
	Go for it!	Forget	
Low			

	Low	High

Effort

Evaluation Decision Matrix

- The person who comes up with the original idea should implement the idea themselves or with their work team. If additional help is needed from maintenance, I.T. etc. the idea originator should oversee the completion of this work.

- Record implemented ideas in an idea log and/or electronically into an idea tracking software package. This IT version is useful as the system grows and can be used as a knowledge database base for intra and cross site spread. Software can also be utilised for automatic metric report generation. Data mining also becomes important once you get to several hundred ideas, to establish trends etc.

- Develop monthly metrics to ensure that the goal of two ideas per month is reached and display the results visually at the Gemba. It is best if the local cell Idea Champion maintains these.

Some metrics to measure success include:

- number of ideas per employee/team
- volume of implemented ideas
- participation rate
- speed of implementation
- % of implemented Vs. non-implemented

If the cycle above flows smoothly the improvement activity will also flow slickly, one idea will lead to another and continuous improvement will translate into improved performance and higher employee engagement.

The future intention is that this cycle will be used hundreds of times daily and simplicity is all! In summary the essentials elements of high performing idea systems are: (a) It is easy to submit ideas; (b) The evaluation process is swift; and (c) feedback is immediate and continual throughout the idea implementation cycle. The effective working of this cycle is imperative if high participation and performance levels are to be accomplished.

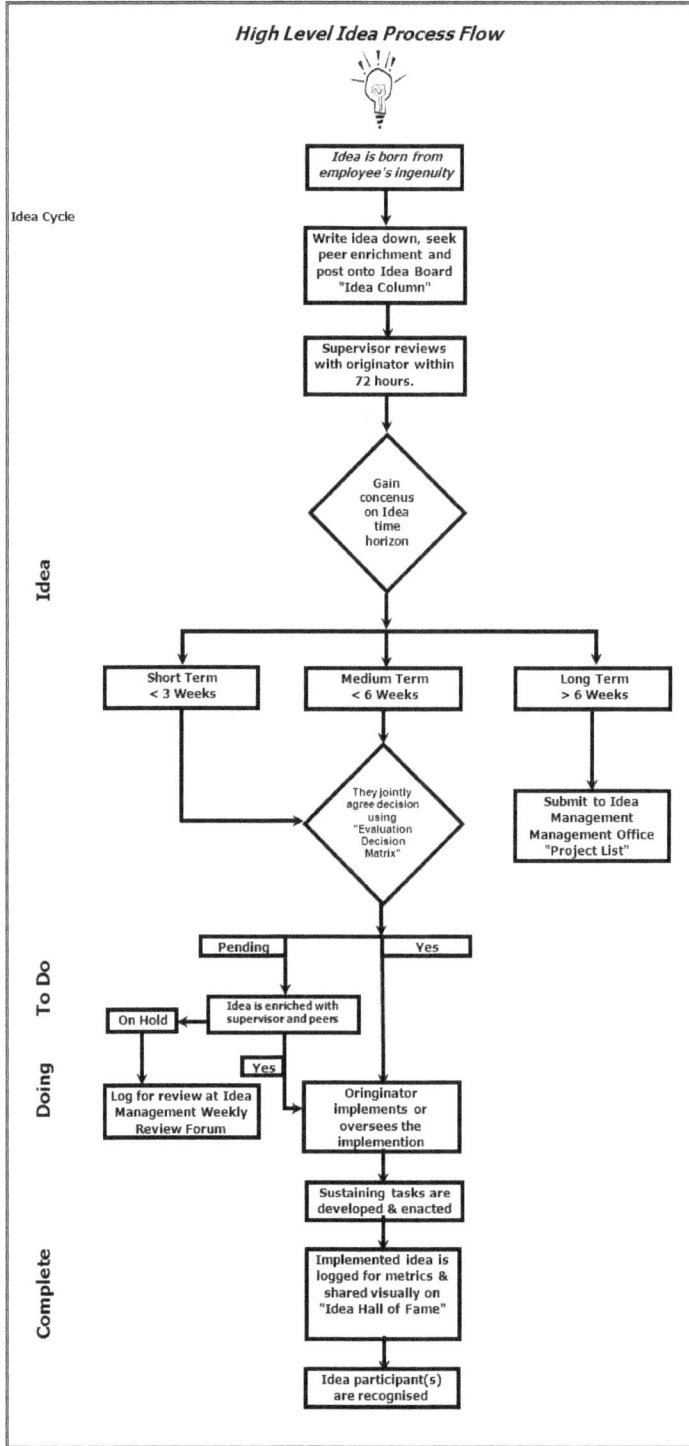

High Level Idea Process Flow

Idea Cycle

Idea is born from employee's ingenuity

Write idea down, seek peer enrichment and post onto Idea Board "Idea Column"

Supervisor reviews with originator within 72 hours.

Gain concenus on Idea time horizon

Idea

Short Term < 3 Weeks

Medium Term < 6 Weeks

Long Term > 6 Weeks

They jointly agree decision using "Evaluation Decision Matrix"

Submit to Idea Management Management Office "Project List"

To Do

Pending

Yes

On Hold

Idea is enriched with supervisor and peers

Yes

Doing

Log for review at Idea Management Weekly Review Forum

Orininator implements or oversees the implemention

Sustaining tasks are developed & enacted

Complete

Implemented idea is logged for metrics & shared visually on "Idea Hall of Fame"

Idea participant(s) are recognised

Idea Process Flow Diagram

IMS Administration

The primary gatekeepers for idea administration are the direct frontline supervisor assisted by the appointed idea champion for each local team. Tasks include:
- monitoring and registering of ideas on the Idea Board
- clarifying ideas and obtaining further information if required
- metric reporting
- promoting and marketing the system
- organising recognition presentations

Budget

One of the most critical elements of a successful system is an adequate budget for idea implementation work, recognition, and promotion. It is good practice to have a rolling budget that can be bumped up if the stream of ideas is greater than anticipated. When setting a budget always keep in mind the significant return on investment that an IMS can deliver. It is not unusual to see ratios of greater than 100:1 return on ideas for some best practice systems, indeed ratios of much larger magnitudes are common! It is worth considering if Workforce Development or HR fund the budget from their training allocation as the IMS is essentially a skills development system and much more powerful than classroom based courses. Some of the most successful systems are lead from the HR function.

Recognition Considerations (see Chapter 3)

Promotion of Ideas

Constant promotion is a key activity of the Idea Management Office.

Strategies to keep the system alive and invigorated include:

- At the outset tailor the message to the audience: market to frontline people as "their" system to make their jobs easier and get them involved in the decision making process; for gaining management support stress the potential financial savings and increased levels of employee engagement.
- Regular features in company newsletters
- Make current business issues as clear as possible to employees so that they can truly be effective in generating ideas (Sander 2005)
- "Idea of the Month" winners and posting plaques of participants on walls
- Posters and brochures at all key locations
- Themed campaigns for selected weeks such as a "Environmental Ideas Week"
- Email and pay check stub advertisement
- Originate or recycle someone else's name or logo - building a brand is so important. You want staff to recognise instantly things that are associated with your scheme – brand all stationary from posters to mugs (Holt 2007)

- Polo shirts with the idea brand logo on them build solidarity – they have an urgency about them and become infectious (adapted from Kelley 2001)
- Metaphors are powerful – example "ideas are like a surgeon" for stimulating say TPM "Spot the Rot" detailed machine inspections and resultant improvement opportunities

"... paying particular attention to how they are advertised and how participation is rewarded ... improves the return on idea capture schemes" (Leach, J., Stride, C., & Woods, S. 2006).

Considerations for IMS Rules

It is wise to define the key words in an IMS – words such as idea, evaluation, recognition etc. This helps avoid later misunderstandings. An example might be an argument over what constitutes an idea over normal day to day tasks. An "Idea" definition might be that, an "Idea" is where you are required to ask permission to go ahead and implement (Denatale 2007).

Submitting your idea signifies giving ownership of the idea and any resultant Intellectual Property etc. to the company. Define who is eligible to participate. Are group or team ideas to be included? Ideas which are not acceptable can include:

- Complaints without constructive solutions

- Subjects related to pay, benefits and promotions

Define the recognition policy and communicate this to the target areas.

Keep your rules as brief and simple as possible. Let the guiding principle be; the fewer the rules the better.

Pilot Implementation

Use an inch wide, mile deep strategy. Run a test pilot in a small area before launching the IMS across the value stream. Use an After Action Review to improve the wider launch roll-out.

IMS Audit

Perform six monthly health assessments of the IMS to highlight areas that are performing well and also to drive action that will strengthen lower performing areas. See adapted ideasUK assessment in (Appendix II) for an example of the audit criteria. The association grades their members idea systems based on final scores against the degree that each of the criterion are present. The grades go from Platinum, Gold, Silver, & Bronze based on performance of the system. It is also good practice for the idea originator to review their implemented ideas, say after six months, to ensure that the gains are held.

Closing Points

Involving employees in idea implementation leads to culture change and a positive work environment where people feel valued and listened to. Often omitted from Lean transformations are the thinking aspects that provide the "adhesive" to holding everything together. A well designed and supported IMS is one of the prime vehicles utilised to close this gap in organisations such as Toyota.

The primary focus of the Kaizen style IMS is on small ideas self-implemented or where implementation is coordinated by the idea originator. Small things done consistently with the right focus create the strongest impact. The finding's from numerous benchmarking visits and interviews undertaken for this chapter validates that the Kaizen technique delivers superior results (morale and financial) in comparison with traditional bureaucratic suggestion schemes.

Counter-intuitively decentralised systems that focused on small ideas and high participation rates delivered financial returns that were typically in the range of ten times greater than traditional style systems that focused mainly on larger ROI ideas. A hybrid approach can be useful for capturing larger and small ideas. The larger ideas are handled by the traditional route and the small ideas locally.

A number of common enablers for successful IMS's were also identified. Management made a clear and visible commitment to everyone that ideas would be taken seriously. Management embraced the role of coach and moved away from the command and control style of supervision. Teach people how to recognise and solve problems. People were coached on the Lean waste types, creativity tools and some of the seven tools of quality such as fishbone causal analysis. Training in these tools will help employees release the "hidden gold" in their heads. Managers allocated time to employees to implement their ideas so that the mass intelligence in the organisation could be tapped. It was stipulated in employee development plans that implementing small ideas was part of their jobs. Submitting ideas was simple, via idea boards and these were reviewed daily by their direct supervisors. Idea Champions were developed in local work teams to stimulate the system and keep it alive. The system was decentralised and employees were given quick constructive feedback and mentoring with overseeing the implementation of their ideas. Peer review helped to ensure that quality ideas were raised and this fostered effective decision making at the lowest level possible. Idea turnaround time was fast. Idea sharing and spreading was encouraged by the top performers. The systems were actively promoted and ideas were pulled by virtue of how the process was designed, that is problems were surfaced continually in a blame free environment. The purpose of the IMS was marketed as a technique to increase people's skills and capabilities. The supervisor was the key gatekeeper and social interaction with the frontlines was paramount as many times people had difficultly articulating their ideas in writing, but could do so verbally if asked. People were also recognised and success celebrated. The most effective form of recognition for ideas was to use them, and credit the people involved. Idea system performance was measured by a few metrics that were needed to know how the system was operating and how it could be improved.

In contrast the average performing organisations had generally centralised systems, and had longer evaluation times stretching into months in some cases. Ideas were raised for other people to implement them, which resulted in multiple hand-offs, poor feedback and little if any involvement by the originator in implementation. This resulted in high rejection rates and hence low participation as people were reluctant to be knocked back. Systems that used monetary rewards based on a % of savings experienced lower performance as sharing duplicate ideas was not encouraged.

Depending on the circumstances centralised systems have their place where organisations may be looking for "breakthrough" or larger ideas through a standardised approach and that expertise is spread over a large geographical area. There are less training and development requirements with this type of system. However if we are engaging in a Lean transformation where multiple small ideas are required to support continual process improvement, this type of system will choke under its own bureaucracy.

Improving the capability of people is perhaps the ultimate purpose for establishing an idea system. Again: if you look after the people their improved competence will return the rewards to the company. In the Lean world this is an absolute necessity as problems are continually exposed. The IMS can allow an organisation to realise the latent and untapped talent pool already within its four walls. The reason for this is subtly captured in the quote below.

> *"If you want one year of prosperity, grow seeds.*
> *If you want ten years of prosperity, grow trees.*
> *If you want one hundred years of prosperity, grow people."*
> *(Liker & Meier 2007)*

Chapter 5

Idea Enablers for Problem Solving and Improvement

"We are continually faced by great opportunities brilliantly disguised as insoluble problems." Lee Iacocca

All of the Lean tools are designed to make the process visible and to enable problem surfacing. Basic Problem solving tools can then be deployed in real time to dissolve these problems when the root cause trails are still hot. This chapter outlines some of these tools that serve as a strong enabler for maximising the potential of idea systems.

Establish Enablers

Walking the Frontlines

The Gemba Walk (also commonly referred to as a waste walk) means to come to the workplace, observe, and understand. It is a first cousin of the Lean Pillar of Respect for People as that no employee or customer wants their time wasted by non value adding tasks. It is a great way to foster interaction between management and the frontlines and to stimulate improvement ideas. Ideally this is a cascaded strategy right down from top managers to the people on the frontlines. It is carried out at predefined frequencies to the point of being a bi-daily activity at the supervisor level. Developing an explicit language for waste gives people a new lens to help them recognise it and hence strive to remove it. For example the management in a hospital ward did not regard walking as a waste, until the Gemba walk identified that poor layout of supplies was contributing to nurses walking five miles per shift. On further analysis this equated to 1 ¼ hours of nursing care time being lost per nurse shift for patients and indeed nurse frustration and fatigue/safety issues because of poor system design.

The power in the Gemba walk lies in:

- Selecting a theme for each walk
- Questioning the team leaders and employees and asking for ideas
- Listening attentively. This is a learning exercise for the manager
- Sharing what you learned as you walk through the area
- Writing a short memo on what you learned and posting it for sharing
- Give the employees stimulators to instigate and implement ideas to embed Lean skill
- Following up to monitor progress

Section Two

Waste Opportunities	Waste Walk Examples	Ideas for Countermeasure
Waiting (for equipment, materials, information, management decision, patients waiting etc)	Patients waiting for Doctors, X-Rays, Fracture Clinics, Nursing Home Beds, Discharge Clearance	*(employees come up with creative ideas to solve the issues raised in the second column)*
Transporting (poor layout, moving patients, supplies etc)	Walking for Linen, Sluice Room, Unplanned Dressing, Trolleys back to Laundry	
Motion (walking, poor ergonomics, stretching, lifting, equipment access etc)	Walking due to existing layout, one photocopier between two wards, "Treasure Hunts" of searching for kit/supplies/who has keys?	
Over-processing (over testing; excessive legacy inspection; multiple entry of data; asking patients more than once etc)	4 hourly OPS (temp, bloods) in some cases, nursing notes, asking patients more than once for personal details etc	
Unnecessary Services (delivering meds before required, unnecessary diagnostic procedures)	Batching all records ahead of time	
Inventory (excess supplies, expired meds etc)	Kanban racks, reduce the inventory levels by 30%	
Work in Progress (patients queuing for equipment, start stop treatment)	Medication nurse being interrupted in the middle of round	
Defects & Rework (workarounds, wrong chart data, items missing, mistakes or near misses not captured and root caused)	Missing items, take chart without leaving a visual cue as to whereabouts, medication mix ups, morphine pump set wrong	
Poor Design (equipment not designed to support ease of use etc)	"Old Style" Med Trolley hurts back, hard to squeeze out wash cream from tube, commode packaging difficult to open	
Human Potential (improvement ideas asked for and locally not implemented, nurses doing jobs outside of their expertise)	Ideas raised and not acted on in a timely manner, nurses forced to do non nursing related tasks	
Environmental Pollution (not following infection control protocols, hazardous chemicals, spills/ leakages & safety issues etc)	Non 100% Compliance to Infection Controls 100% of Time	

Unnecessary Overhead (large equipment, ward, larger equipment than necessary, etc)	One of the stores is redundant	
Power & Energy (oxygen on at idle bays, air leaks, idle machines powered on, lighting , PC's and printers left on)	Old style tungsten bulbs in use, lights left on in locked supply stores	
Wasted Materials (supplies, food, etc)	Tablets spilled on floor, also a fall hazard	
IT Systems (issues with computers; scanners; etc)	No Internet access on Ward, No Color printer - inducing long walks, shared photocopier	
Culture (non improvement mentality, blame culture, patient first, comfortable to report problems and non conformances)	Staff reluctant to raise issues from last night at shift hand over due to fear culture	

Gemba Walk Waste Card (Healthcare Example)

Having an explicit language gives a lens that enables associates to see waste. By deeply embedding the 16 wastes "language", organisations see opportunities through this lens that were not previously apparent. The waste card should be familiar to all in the facility and carried on Gemba walks to provoke improvement ideas.

Implemented Idea Booklets

Showing people examples from Kaizen booklets raises their degree of belief that they too can self-implement ideas. These booklets are simply a collection of implemented idea cards (see below). Over time these booklets can be expanded as more ideas are implemented to form significant idea training books. Posting implemented ideas on the wall, sometimes termed a "Wall of Recognition" gives acknowledgement to your employees for making the improvement. Idea booklets also help spread ideas throughout the company.

Kaizen Idea Cards

Ideas are captured by writing them down on Kaizen Cards as per example below. The idea is written down, concisely detailing the before and after situation along with the effect. The idea originator fills in their name and classifies the area of improvement such as "better process", along with a quick educated guess of cost savings from predefined guidelines. It is also good practice to include pictures of the before and after condition to enhance clarity. Finally the status of the idea progress is stated and the card is posted on an idea board for sharing.

Kaizen Idea Card		
Idea #	Cell/Line Ref:	
Date	Originator	Supervisor
Picture/Sketch of Current condition		Picture/Sketch of Target Condition
Description of Current condition		Description of Target Condition
Team Member/Supervisor To Complete Together		
Estimated Impact		What We Learned By Implementing This Idea
Impact Verified By		Yokoten/Leverage Opportunities

Kaizen Idea Card

Lean Tools to Surface Problems

Lean tools stimulate people to think creatively. Standard Work, Poka Yoke, Visual Management, 5S, SMED, and TPM are some examples. The six improvement categories discussed in Chapter 1 outline different approaches to making improvements. Improvement can be either passive or in reaction to issues or it can be driven by the management and/or design of the organisation and its processes. Improvement can be further broken down into small step by step incremental improvement or breakthrough "event" type improvement.

Some Examples:

Standard work - This provides the current best known way to do the job. Lean uses the term "standardised work" to apply to a particular job done by a particular associate. For example a left-handed, colour-blind, short person would certainly have a different method to a right-handed, normal vision, tall person. The current known best practice or sequence of activities that minimises waste is established in co-operation with the person who does the work directly. It is not fixed in stone – a better way is always possible. It ensures that activities are executed consistently with minimal variation. Standard Work Sheets incorporate procedures, inventory levels, and targeted performance times.

Note that usually less than half of activities are what are referred to as "Key Points" in TWI (Training Within Industry) methodology. A "key point" is something that makes or breaks the job, makes it easier to do, or involves health and safety aspects. Reasons for each key point must be known. Note also that TWI methodology does not specify times. The rate of work is derived, not specified. To over-standardise is a mistake.

People will follow standard work when they are involved in developing it through Kaizen and idea implementation as they then share the understanding of why the standard is there. Hence they are involved in the thinking, not just following some blind sequence like a machine.

Standardisation does not remove the need for creativity – it spreads this need and "temporary best known way" throughout the company (Robinson & Stern 98). Any deviations from the standard work charts must be viewed as opportunities for improvement and idea implementation. Of course this implies that management must nurture the creation of a blame free environment, and this sends out the message that they welcome the proactive submission of problems. This must be supported both verbally and by their actions. Of course, if employees see people being punished for highlighting issues the idea system will die. A mistake board is a good visual method for people to share mistakes that they have made for others to learn from and come forward with improvement countermeasures.

Poke Yoke or Error-Proofing - This is a technique that prevents mistakes. An everyday example is the domestic three pin plug; it can be inserted only one way. People should strive to design the work procedures using poke yoke devices so that it is easy to do the right thing and hard if not impossible to do the wrong thing as in the three pin plug example above. This opens up all kinds of creative pathways for employees to contribute ideas.

Visual Management - We are born as visual creatures; indeed 80% of the brain is dedicated to visual processing. We need to recognise and incorporate this fact into our workplace design. The main reasons for visual management are:

- To make problems immediately visible
- To help workers and management stay in direct contact with the gemba (frontlines)
- To clarify targets for improvement
- Promote communication and employee involvement through improvement ideas
- Make everyone's jobs easier and less stressful
- Recognise achievements and improvements

Visual Management: Using the techniques below quickly to detect & correct abnormal conditions
Visual Measures: Real time data that informs employees on how they're performing
Visual Display: All needed items in area, tools, SOP's, spec. limits, available at a glance
Workplace Organisation (5S):   Area is designed for optimum performance and safety

Four Levels of a Visual Management

The purpose for visual controls is to focus on the process and make it easy to contrast intended versus achieved performance, in essence to make visual the things you would not normally see and to stimulate improvement ideas. The supervisor's role is to facilitate resolution of problems that interfere with the associates' ability to run smoothly all day. Visual charts tell the story of where the supervisor needs to step in and solicit improvement ideas. Instead of real-time indicators of current performance, it is typical to see weekly, monthly or even quarterly reports. These may indicate where outcomes are not as desired, but rarely provide enough detail to formulate a plan of action for improvement on a daily basis. One hallmark of managing in a Lean culture is quick response to deviations from the standard process. Two elements are required to realise this in the workplace— a defined agreed upon standard (that works and is followed by all) and a method to determine quickly departures from that standard. Without these as a foundation, employees cannot make informed decisions to react in a timely manner to bring the process back into control.

Visual management is the driver for communicating the process, the targets, the performance, and the desired response. With visual management, a quick walk through the workplace is all that is needed to determine the status of the workplace, good day, bad day.... and if intervention is required. Hence organisations must strive to design a workplace that almost talks to you, where problems become immediately apparent. Hence you can manage by sight.

By responding to issues at the time they occur and asking "Why?" five times, root causes can usually be quickly identified as the root cause(s) trail is still warm and process corrections can be made in relative real time before the problem escalates.

5S - This is the synthesis of many small proactive improvements leading to a more efficient and safer work area. A good 5S training program sensitises people to all kinds of ideas and ways they can become more productive. The five S's are Sort (putting things in order), Set-in-Order (arranging things efficiently), Shine (preventing problems by inspecting and/or disinfecting and generally keeping things clean), Standardise (allotting time for first 3 S's everyday), and Sustain (showing discipline, following the rules). Anytime it takes people more than a few seconds to find something, they should ask themselves why? A decade after Toyota Kentucky began 5S training, managers say that employees were still coming up with approximately 6,500 5S ideas alone each year. The beauty of ideas surfaced via a 5S theme is that they can usually be implemented quickly and have a positive effect both on productivity and employee "misery factors". An example of a "misery factor" could be struggling to cut ten cables ties on a container of parts where a simple clip device would have been adequate to secure the contents.

5S is often viewed as a straight forward housekeeping practice. However the deeper underlying intent is to develop a team member's knowledge and responsibility about their immediate work area. 5S becomes an ongoing practice to help people think about how their work area is laid out and arranged, and for them to act on all the small ideas that can make it better, safer, more ergonomic, and easier and less stressful to work in.

5S is also an extremely powerful waste reduction tactic. If you consider that every employee performs thousands of tasks per week in each of their areas and seconds saved on each of the wastes below can add significantly to the bottom line. Especially when multiplied by hundreds of people in the company each and everyday of the year!

5S is a commonly used starting point on the Lean journey as it is very employee centric and improvements are visible very quickly in the area. Jane Norman of PKP Inc. uses the analogy of mowing the lawn to describe the impact of 5S, an immediate and distinct improvement in the work environment.

Waste	Ward Example
Transport	Equipment moved multiple times
Inventory	Excess medical supplies on racks
Motion	Extra walking due to poor layout of supplies
Waiting	Patient waiting in pain as nurse searches for correct painkiller
Overproduction	Only the correct amount of stock held
Overprocessing	Patient been asked more than once during visit for their details
Defects	Drug mix ups due to poor layout; contamination issues
Others	
Culture	Improved morale and participation
Safety	Major enabler – loose cables, trip hazards, infection etc
Abnormal Conditions	Immediately become apparent and real time resolution
Power & Energy	Defective equipment captured during 3rd S (Shine – inspect)
Wasted Materials	Four packs of alcohol wipes opened in one area
Computers	Find any file on PC in 30 seconds

Hospital Visual for alerting employees to the real purpose and power of 5S; and to stimulate idea possibilities

Section Two

Quick Changeover (QCO) - This is usually instigated by management to enable strategic issues such as lead time and inventory reduction. The principles behind quick changeover can be taught in several hours and result in employees thinking of all kinds of ideas that they might not otherwise. With enough ideas, the length of time it takes to change machines or operating rooms over from performing one operation to beginning another can be reduced from hours to a few minutes. A great example of quick changeover is the Formula 1 pit-stop service. The deeper purpose of QCO is to provide the capability to do more changeovers (not reduce the time changing over) hence moving towards the aspirational goal of one piece flow.

Total Productive Maintenance (TPM) - Another example TPM, involves an aggressive measurement, "overall equipment effectiveness (OEE)," to highlight problems that most organisations would normally miss. With the advent of TPM, managers accustomed to reporting flattering efficiency levels—above 90 percent, say—find themselves sheepishly reporting overall equipment effectiveness levels of maybe 30 to 40 percent. Opportunities for improvement that they had not being seen before become quite obvious. OEE is comprised of an aggregate metric which is:

Availability x Performance Rate x Quality Rate

These are evaluated according to six losses which are

- Breakdowns (availability)
- Excessive set-up time and adjustments (availability)
- Idling & Minor Stoppages (performance rate)
- Reduced Speed (performance rate)
- Reduced Yield (quality rate)
- Start-up losses (quality rate)

The above losses represent many opportunities to capture frontline expertise and ideas for improvement.

Hourly Boards - Known by many as the most powerful Lean improvement tool! An example of "Target vs. Actual" management on the frontlines is an hourly board showing current versus expected status for all processes. These are most effective if they are maintained by the associates working the processes, manually at predetermined intervals. Reasons for misses are recorded and used for real time problem solving and improvement idea implementation. An example from a manufacturing plant is a flip chart at the workplace divided into hourly intervals and the team member updates this on an hourly basis and writes in the actual units produced and the delta against the target if this arises. If there is a negative delta the reason for this is recorded and corrective action is performed in almost real time to correct the situation for the next hour. This has the power of stimulating the thinking and brainpower of the team to put forward improvement ideas for experimentation. A hospital example would be a board detailing the planned number of patients scheduled to see a physician per hour at an outpatient's clinic versus the actual number seen. If the queue is expanding after an hourly update on the board a countermeasure could be to redeploy an extra physician for the next hour to clear the backlog.

Other Lean Idea Surfacers:

- Value Stream Mapping (ideas to realise the future state)
- Work balance charts displayed in cells, helping with work allocation
- Pitch misses recorded on pitch board (schedule attainment)
- Red tags are placed on equipment needing attention
- Shrinking intra process inventory to see if issues are surfaced
- SPC and other performance variation data should be kept at the Gemba
- Cleaning is checking and visual sweeping
- 3P or production preparation process is a methodology that requires the cell or layout team, including front line staff, to develop several alternatives for each process step and to evaluate each alternative
- Waste posters with specific organisational examples in every cell
- Value Add – Non Value Add Time Ladder
- One great trick to develop employees' ideas is to tap into the lunchtime conversations. What do your employees complain about over lunch? Many times they talk about problems that everyone knows about except for management. Managers would learn a lot if they could listen to employees talking at lunch. This can be achieved by giving a team of people a lunch voucher on a monthly basis and having an open air lunch with their management team where constructive critique is welcomed from the outset.
- Taiichi Ohno felt that if we stood in the circle for an hour watching the workplace, and asking "why?" better ideas would come to us. He realised that new thoughts and new technologies do not come out of the blue; they come from a true understanding of the process. Another variant aims to observe 30 small things you could improve in the first half hour and then kick-off implementation of these in the second half of the hour!
- People come with built-in noise detection, vision, odour, and vibration equipment, their five senses! Use these precious capabilities and get associates to report anything unusual (using the IMS as an upward communication device)
- Bottleneck resources should be a pull for improvement ideas
- Ask what operations make no sense. This informal attention helps people to open up.

Basic Problem Solving Tools

Problem solving is the essence of Lean, Toyota has a saying, "Find a problem, fix a problem, and stop it from coming back".

Training Within Industry (TWI) Program

TWI is a four stage program for training employees:

- How to do the task – called Job Instruction (JI)
- How continually to look for ways to improve the task – called Job Methods (JM)
- Guidance for treating and managing people with respect is detailed in the Job Relations program (JR) so that the effectiveness of both the JI and JM programs are maximised. This relates to the Respect for People Pillar.

- Later, TWI added Job Safety

It must be emphasised that these are seen as a system or set – to be mutually reinforcing – not as four stand-alone activities.

As detailed in next paragraph with JM, Step One defines and breaks down the job and Step Two calls to "Question Every Detail" of the job. Step Three develops a new method and Step Four applies the new method. Applying the method means communicating it to everyone, documenting the new method in a way that it will be sustained, and putting the method to use. JM is a strong reason why many Japanese companies have such a high number of improvements (not just ideas) implemented by their employees. Often, employees have many good ideas that would improve productivity, but they do not know how to implement them. When an idea is proposed, the procedure in place is cumbersome or ineffective for sustaining changes. JM training offers a simple four step analytical method for an employee to take action to make changes that result in an easier job. When the intention is to make their own jobs easier; people are intrinsically motivated to use the method and don't have to be prodded to make improvements (adapted from Dinero 2005). JM was the core program for idea systems evolving into what became known as Lean. Indeed the entire Kaizen movement is strongly attributed to this program.

HOW TO IMPROVE - JOB METHODS

This is a practical plan to help produce greater quantities of quality products in less time by making the **best use** of the **Manpower, Machines and Materials, now available.**

STEP 1 BREAK DOWN THE JOB
1. List **all** details of the job **exactly** as done in the **Current Method.**
2. Be sure details include everything:
   - Material Handling
   - Machine Work
   - Hand Work

STEP 2 QUESTION EVERY DETAIL
1. Use these types of questions:
   WHY is it necessary?
   WHAT is its purpose?
   WHERE should it be done?
   WHEN should it be done?
   WHO is best qualified to do it?
   HOW is the "best way" to do it?
2. Question the following at the same time:
   Materials, Machines, Equipment, Tools,
   Product Design, Workplace Layout,
   Movement, Safety, Housekeeping

STEP 3 DEVELOP THE NEW METHOD
1. **ELIMINATE** unnecessary details
2. **COMBINE** details when practical
3. **REARRANGE** details for better sequence
4. **SIMPLIFY** all necessary details
   To make the job easier and safer to do:

- Put materials, tools and equipment into the **best position** and **within convenient reach** for the operator
- Use **gravity feed hoppers** or **drop delivery chutes** wherever possible
- Make effective use of **both hands**

5. Work out your ideas WITH OTHERS
6. WRITE UP the proposed new method

STEP 4 APPLY THE NEW METHOD
1. SELL your proposal to the boss
2. SELL the new method to the operators
3. Get FINAL APPROVAL of all concerned on Safety, Quality, Quantity, Cost, etc.
4. PUT the new method TO WORK. Use it until a **better** way is developed.
5. Give CREDIT where credit is due.

(Source: transcribed from TWI Job Methods Card detailed in Graup and Wrona, 2006)

A3 Problem Solving

A3 problem solving is a methodology used to align people and mentor them in problem solving. It works through the PDSA cycle and as the name suggests is confined to a single sheet of A3 paper for maximum conciseness and clarity. This also reduces management communication time and forces deep thinking. It enables a deep focus on the problem through its structured approach and encourages collaborative team based conversations about the problem. It is common for A3's to contain both hand written text and sketches. Adequate time should be spent at the outset on properly clarifying and defining the problem, only then should the team proceed to the next steps. A3 is not a linear form of problem solving and teams should move backwards and forward through the steps to update the sheet and maximise learning. A3 problem should be performed at the Gemba involving those who work in the process; this enables the maximum surfacing of relevant ideas for successful problem resolution. Spread of successful problem solving work through the organisation is greatly enhanced by the concise one page format of this methodology. It is a great template for implementing some improvement ideas and ensuring that they are tested and verified for effectiveness. The challenge is to work diligently through all the eight steps, it is common practice to skip steps 1 and 2 and stop at step 5 or 6, hence sustaining issues arise! One of the major building blocks in the creation of a Lean culture is for management to commit to following **ALL 9** steps of this process for problem solving and idea implementation. Over time the goal should be that the 9 steps evolve to be the cognitive way that people in the organisation think in their heads about issues, not just on paper.

1. Clarify the Problem (PLAN) Ensure that we are working on the right problem!	4. Root Cause Analysis 5 Why Investigation Direct Cause(s) Root Cause(s)	7. Monitor Results & Process (STUDY) Verify that the countermeasures have been effective
2. Breakdown the Problem Locate the point of cause Cause Effect Investigate Define the problems to tackle	5. Develop Countermeasures Plan to test changes	8. Standardise and Spread Successful Processes (ACT) Leverage the gains and opportunity for improvement
3. Target Setting What are we trying to accomplish?	6. See Countermeasures Through (DO) Coordinated and speedy implementation	9. Reflection What went well? What could we improve for the next cycle? What insights were learned?

Example of A3 Format

Process Mapping

The process map lists every step that is involved in the manufacture of a product or service delivery. There are special symbols to indicate "operation", "delay", "move", "storage", and "inspect". It helps to identify waste and is a good communication tool for stimulating ideas. It is also powerful for standardising processes after improvement. The mapping should be done at the Gemba, not in an office (if we are not mapping an office process!). Once the chart is complete the individual steps can be brainstormed into those that add value, those that are pure waste which should be eliminated as soon as possible, and those which are necessary non value added (needed to support the process in the short term). It is a great tool for generating ideas about alternative solutions to achieve the purpose of the process. An enhancement to the basic map is a person-machine map which highlights what the person is doing during equipment cycle time and helps to uncover wasteful time gaps. A good analogy to obtain input for this type of chart is to ask if you would sit and watch your washing machine clean your clothes for the full cycle! Another map often combined with process mapping is the spaghetti diagram that can be used to show associate and material travel distances and convoluted flow. Service blue print mapping is often used in the service environment to document the customers experience in dealing with the service offering – another great source of ideas!

Six Honest Serving Men

"I knew six honest serving men, they taught me all I knew; their names are what, why and when, and where and how and who".
(from Rudyard Kipling)

This technique is useful for integrating with process mapping as outlined below. It is also incorporated in the TWI Job Methods procedure described above.

5 W's & 1 H	Thinking Questions
What?	What is done?
Why?	What is the purpose?
	Is the purpose accomplished? How do we know?
	Why is it necessary?
	What if it were eliminated?
	What would make it unnecessary?
Where?	Where is it performed?
	What alternate location is feasible?
	Can it be reorganised?
When?	What other order would work?
	Can it be merged with something else?
	What are the implications of other sequences?
Who?	Who performs the activity?
	Who else could do it?
How?	What other method could be employed?
	What other technologies exist?

Six Honest Serving Men

Fishbone Diagram
This is a visual team involvement tool to brainstorm out possible causes of a problem. The potential contributing causes are written in the diagram. It is common to use the six "M's" to label the initial bones that are Man (person), Machine, Methods, Materials, Measurement and Mother Nature. It is great for getting employees involved and contributing improvement ideas to issues (not all necessary related to problems but for opportunities as well). This is used in the A3 Problem Solving Process.

Tally Chart
Simple but powerful, placed next to the process step; this is used to check the cause of issues. Useful for identifying trends such as particular day of the week, shift etc. Use Fishbone diagram and Pareto to help determine this.

Defect	Monday	Tuesday	Wednesday	Thursday	Friday	Total
Solder	I	II		I		4
Part	II		I	II	I	6
Not-to-Print	III	II	I	III	II	11
Timing		I	I		I	3
Other		I				1

Tally Chart

Section Two

Pareto Diagram
This principle is named after Alfredo Pareto an economist who noted that a few people controlled most of a nation's wealth. This has been called "the single most powerful management technique of all time". It gives recognition to the fact that a small number of problems (< 20%) account for a large percentage (> 80%) of the effect of the overall number of problems. That is, the "vital few" cause you 80% of the pain! Get after these first before the "trivial many".

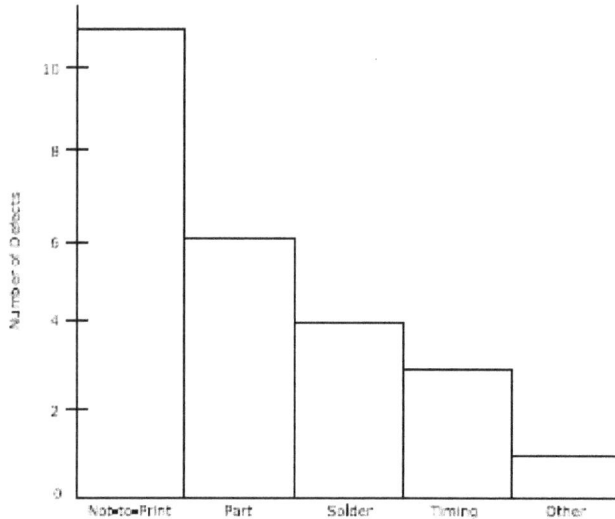

Pareto Diagram collated from a Tally Sheet

Measles Chart or Scatter Plot
Each defect occurrence is plotted on an existing defective part or engineering drawing at the location where the problem occurs. If the accumulation density is concentrated in one area it gives an excellent indication where the problem lies. Some companies use this method to identify which areas in the organisation are generating the most ideas for improvement.

Gap Analysis
This is powerful for alerting the employees to envision what is possible and hence create tension to improve via constructive dissatisfaction.

- What is the gap? (What are we trying to improve/accomplish?)
- What's preventing us from meeting our target? (A fishbone diagram shows causes contributing to the gap)
- What are the causes in order of performance? (Pareto ranks the causes)
- What actions will address the most important causes?

Socratic Questioning

Socrates' goal was to compel his students to think deeply and learn, by challenging the clarity and completeness of their thinking. The questioning approach is fundamental to Lean thinking. As Goldratt says, every time you tell a person something you remove the opportunity of the person finding it out for themselves. It is a form of disrespect. By contrast, asking "What do you think?" means the leader is a teacher. The underlying message is that I value your opinion. A benevolent cycle results: people feel good and they get involved, which makes them feel better. The result is that companies like Toyota get millions of improvement ideas from team members.

A good question invites and provokes creative critical thinking.

Guidelines for asking good questions:

- ask open ended questions, not yes or no questions
- just ask one question at a time; you'll get a more complete answer
- don't interrupt, or put words in the person's mouth.
- listen by trying to put yourself in the shoes of the speaker
- use common vocabulary
- ask unrestrained what ifs?, to open up to possibilities
- ask "if you owned this company what would you do to improve it?"
- ask "what could I do as a leader to serve you better?"
- and ask, "what do I need to do next to make your job better and easier?"

Five Why Analysis

Supervisors can use the five whys to encourage their people to think about the true causes of problems or waste and ask for ideas to solve the issue.

Problem statement:

We only made 900 widgets. Target is 1200.
Why?
The loader stopped.
Why?
It was overloaded and a fuse blew.
Why?
The arm wasn't adequately lubricated.
Why?
The lubrication pump was blocked up.
Why?
The dispenser on the pump was damaged.
Why?
Dirt and grit entered the pump shaft.
Why?
The pump motor was designed without a filter.

You can have as many levels of "Whys?" as the situation demands. To test the last core root cause, work your way back up the "Why?" ladder asking "therefore" to verify if each of the "Whys?" holds true. In practice, each "Why?" often leads to several possibilities. You may therefore have to prioritise, go down one branch, and then return to the branching point to explore other possibilities.

Chapter 6

Pit Stop Accelerated Idea Generation Workshop

This chapter lists the main outline steps for running a Pit Stop event. The purpose of the chapter is to give a sense of the steps and resources required to run accelerated idea workshops in an organisation.

Bernie Sander of Innovation Transfer developed the Pit Stop Idea Generation Workshop. This workshop demonstrates within a week the tremendous power of tapping into the ideas of the organisation's employees.

The intent of this workshop is to show management the potential power in creating a culture of continually harnessing employee ideas. It also enables management to see the power of idea systems in terms of engaging and involving employees in decision making, and up-skilling. In conjunction with this management gets a sense of the cost savings that can be realised for their organisation. This process is extremely useful at the outset or pilot stage of implementing a permanent IMS into your organisation. Also it can be utilised as a mechanism to revitalise existing systems. The ultimate goal remains that employees become conscious of problems and opportunities and that both putting forward and implementing ideas becomes a part of the normal day to day culture.

What is PiT-Stop?

As in PiT-Stops during Formula One races, problems are identified by the drivers (employees) and quickly reported. To stay in the race, these problems need to be addressed. The name PiT-Stop also stands symbolically for the speed of the process – problems are brought to light, visualised and clustered into common themes. Decision-making and problem-solving follow at speed. In the end everyone profits - employees as well as management.

"The true secret of success lies in enthusiasm."
Walter Chrysler

PiT-Stop is based on the Kaizen Philosophy

1. Go to GEMBA (Place of Work)
This means: moving away from the dependency on "ideas must be delivered" to actively getting problems, opportunities and ideas from employees.
2. Seek MUDA (Waste)
This means: Creating awareness of the "waste" in daily business.
3. Make KAIZEN (Improving the Good)
This means: Keeping the improvement process in action.

What does PiT-Stop deliver?

- Employee Participation and Involvement
- Motivation
- Process Optimisation
- Savings Potential
- Social Competence
- Goal Achievement
- Knowledge Transfer

The 70% Thesis

- 70% of employees have never submitted a suggestion
- 70% of employees can identify a problem yet have no solution
- 70% of employees can identify the problem yet cannot formulate a cost-benefit analysis
- 70% of employees simply work according to their job description
- 70% of employees have never been asked at their place of work about existing problems

The Wager

In a 15 minute personal interview an employee will name on average 3 concrete problems. On every interview day between 100K and 200K of local currency benefit potential is identified through the problems and ideas of employees. Typical return on investment is 20:1.

Framework for Success Time Table, Responsibilities Internal Communication	**Preparation**
Training of the Facilitators Interviews at the Workplace Collecting Problems	**Problem Finding**
Problem Documentation Structuring, Validation Ascertain the Priorities	**Problem Structuring**
Development of Solutions Facilitated Teamwork for Specific Problems	**Problem Solving**
Closing Presentation, Certification, Recognition, Reporting, Securing Sustainability	**Conclusion and Follow Up**

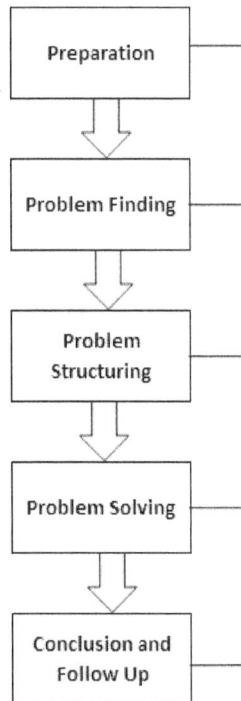

Coordination and Controlling

The Process Milestones

- Employees are asked directly at their place of work about existing problems.
- The problems are documented and the ideas and issues are visually clustered and structured on a problem chart using an affinity diagram. All the information is simultaneously recorded electronically.
- Management and subject matter experts immediately decide on what measures and next steps to take. Decision making tools are used for this purpose. All monetary potential is evaluated in local currency on an annualised basis.
- Small teams develop solutions for specific problems using a facilitated problem solving methodology. The complete PiT-Stop workshop results are presented to senior management as part of the final day wrap-up.

Role of Senior Executive and Management

- They bring all responsible parties and resources to the table and set out the goals and framework for success.
- Through personal support and flexibility they become the promoters for the action days.
- Determine the hourly amount for the labour time saving calculations.

Success Criteria

- A project manager is designated to lead the action days. They are available full time over the week.
- Communication is timely and concise before, after, and indeed during the event.
- Comprehensive documentation and checklists support the local team in their preparations.
- Detailed set-up procedures ensure the success of the action days.

Project Leader/Coordinator

Should be personally present and flexible
Should inform all involved employees of required preparations as early as possible
Should plan for an extensive follow-up to the action days

Preparation Requirements:

Administrator: set up meeting in peoples calendars
Facility Management: room requirements and set-up
Targeted Department: What do they expect? What happens with the ideas and problems?
Interviewers: What to expect? How long will it take? Can it lead to overtime?
Assistants: When will you be needed?
Management: When will the problems and ideas received be evaluated?
Subject Matter Experts: When will they be required (have them on-call) as part of the problem-solving teams?
Work Council/Unions: When can the activities lead to overtime?
Health and Safety: Will security clearance areas be visited? Are photographs permitted?
Canteen: When will refreshments and meals be required?
Personnel: Will non-regulatory entry requirements be required?

Facilitators: When will they be trained and when will they be deployed?
External Facilitators: Will require names of all interviewers and problem-solving facilitators, a floor layout, an organization chart, information about work shift hours and reporting requirements
Room Requirements and Refreshments
The closer to the designated department the better
Avoid room changes during the action days
Tables and chairs for all participants in U-form or island set-up
Refreshments in the cafeteria, canteen but preferably in the action centre
Hot and cold drinks all day

Problem Finding – The Interviews

Why Interviews?
- Problems are best formulated where they originate or show themselves.
- "Go to GEMBA" – "go to the place of origin" as per the Kaizen philosophy.
- Every employee knows of problems slash opportunities at their workplace.
- Every employee has ideas to contribute.
- Through the personal interviews the requirement that employees must bring ideas up themselves is removed.
- Interviews assume the role of actively asking for ideas. This brings success.

The Advantages of Interviews

- In a familiar environment talking is much easier.
- Work is not interrupted much.
- The employee can directly show the problem.
- Employees don't have to formulate and record issues
- The problems of employees do not get filtered through management.
- More appreciation and respect is demonstrated towards the employee
- The interview teams are coached to follow a checklist of specially formulated entry level questions. This makes the first steps easy. Examples of questions include:

  - Is anything a hazard?
  - Do you get complaints from customers?
  - Do you run out of supplies?
  - Is the product inconsistent?
  - Is time lost waiting?
  - Is there waste?
  - Does a rule seem silly?
  - Is energy wasted?
  - Could cheaper materials be used?
  - Do jobs have to be repeated?
  - Is anything too small?
  - Is anything too big?
  - Is something you do unsafe?
  - Does something annoy you?
- Two people facilitate a team. One asks while the other listens attentively and writes the answers on a pre-designed interview form. The formula is simple: "four ears – one mouth".

- With selected questions the interviewers trigger the "awareness of waste". The workplace is looked at through different eyes. Current known best practice or standards are challenged.
- The annual costs of poor performance are estimated in time or material usage with the help of simple formulas.

Typical Findings

- In Production Environments: over production, poor material usage, energy wastage, unnecessary setup times, high failure rates, waiting times, etc.
- In Service Environments: long delivery times, documentation errors, poor information flow, bureaucratic processes, redundant sources of material, etc

Frequently Asked Questions about Problem Finding

- Why are there always two interviewers?
  Four eyes and ears hear and see more than just two. The interview also goes much quicker.
- Does one not receive many duplicate ideas when all employees within a department or division are asked?
  Only approx. 10% of the mentioned problems are truly identical. Besides that, you also reach the less expressive employees, who otherwise would seldom say anything.
- Are the estimates of time and monetary value not highly imprecise?
  The estimates allow for clear priority-setting later in the process. They transmit a real sense of the magnitude of the problem. Therein lies their true worth.
- Why does the interview take place at the workplace?
  At the employee's place of work – in their home environment – they feel secure and there is hardly any interruption to their work. The visit expresses a genuine respect in and value towards the employee.

The interviewers write the key information collected through the interviews on coloured problem cards for maximal visual clarity. The problem description begins with a word that depicts the need for action: "unnecessary ...", "wrong ...", "unclear ...", "unclean ..." etc. Only one problem is recorded on each card. All cards receive a unique number.

Problem Structuring by Clusters

- The cards are organised and allotted to clusters (themed problem areas) that are displayed on pin boards, that act as effective "problem charts".

Typical Clusters
- Problem Types (ex. Material, Energy, Risks etc.)
- Departments (ex. Purchasing, Production, Sales etc.)
- Work Stations (ex. Production Areas, Product Lines, Warehouse Sections etc.)
- Cost Centres (ex. Information Technology, Administration etc.)

Through "clustering" the problems are arranged in logical entities. This enables ease of overview and permits practical handling and assigning of accountability for the next steps of the process. All data collected and decisions made are recorded live in a pre-prepared excel spreadsheet.

Frequently Asked Questions about Problem Structuring

- That looks like a lot of paperwork. How are you supposed to work with all the information?
  All the information is collected live on an electronic database.
- Is the data entry point not a bottleneck?
  When more than 5 interview teams are active, then a second data entry person works in parallel.
- Why does everything need to be written on cards when it will be captured electronically anyway?
  The problem cards deliver one major objective: a good overview - through the posting of the cards, the magnitude of the problems and the multitude of opportunities becomes visible.
- How can one get a grip on this flood of problems?
  Ensure that the clusters remain manageable. The manager responsible for each cluster must be able to assign accountability and process the workload within their daily business. Otherwise there is no end result. Once the problems are recognised, managers and subject matter experts determine the next steps which can include:
    - Person responsible for the problem resolution
    - Priority of the problem
    - Type of problem solving method (ex. PiT-Stop problem solving teams)
    - Date for problem resolution

The historical breakdown of these idea workshops are approximately:

- 10% Just-Do-Its (are immediately solvable)
- 10% quick wins-fast money (are implementable within 30-90 days)
- 30% of all problems are ideally suited for facilitated problem solving teams
- 10% are related to necessary maintenance and repairs
- 40% are either mid and long-term solutions or to be assigned to existing projects

Problem Solving

30% of problems are addressed via Problem Solving in Teams (PiT):

- The selected problems are precisely defined. This minimises the degree of complexity.
- The trained facilitators lead 3 to 7 participants through the problem solving session.
- Using this methodology the employees develop quick, efficient, well-managed solutions and practical implementation measures.
- The method allows for solutions to be formulated within one hour.
- 80-95% of the developed solutions are implemented

Advantages

- Problems are primarily worked on where they occur and are solved by those, who are directly implicated by them. This frees up managers for other tasks.

- Over time all employees are involved in the search for and in the implementation of solutions. This requires entrepreneurial thinking.
- And through it all, the comprehensive training of the local facilitators is important to the success of the method.

Problem Solving Ground Rules

Team Play Rules

- Meetings start on time
- Everyone works together actively
- Everyone listens and lets the other finish their thoughts
- Only one person talks at a time
- No personal criticism
- No hierarchy of people, just ideas

Brainstorming Rules

- No criticism – no comments – no killer phrases
- As many ideas as possible
- Quantity instead of Quality – don't suppress any ideas
- Be creative – speculation is allowed
- Openness towards the other team members
- Be encouraged by other's ideas – hitchhiking is welcomed

Frequently Asked Questions about Problem Solving

- How can you assign so many problems and determine so many countermeasures in such a short space of time?
  External support is great at the outset to provide guidance and drive through the implementation of a large number of ideas.
- How does this problem solving integrate into the normal daily work culture?
  This new way of dealing with problems must become a part of the culture of the organisation. This is where the senior executive team and management are also called upon to break down barriers and roadblocks. They must create the latitude and the time for employees to make it happen. Internally trained facilitators are invaluable to ensure that the process builds and gains momentum.

Recommendations for Sustainability of Ideas

- Ensure that sufficient time and the right people and resources are dedicated to the implementation.
- Make the reporting of the results a fixed element of your meetings.
- Allow the trained facilitators to continue interviews and build more employees into internal facilitators.
- Give employees the time to actively participate in PiT-Stop problem solving sessions.
- Do internal marketing for the action days – before and after.
- Establish key metrics and signal the ongoing success through short update meetings.

- Showcase the activities continuously through billboards, Continuous Improvement Process (CIP) displays, internal magazines and the intranet.
- Say thank you to all active participants for their accomplishments. The recognition practices of an organization show whether the heart is there where the goals lie.

Special thanks to Bernie Sander for providing his workshop material. He developed the Pit-Stop methodology and runs this event with great success worldwide. He can be contacted at:bsander@innovationtransfer.com and www.innovationtransfer.com

Section Four

The main focus of the text up to this point has being about releasing the potential and ideas of the frontline employees. Imai's Kaizen Flag concept also calls for the provision of time for Innovation. In the next chapter we explore the broader field of creativity and innovation to provide the reader with an appreciation for the macro view. Hence the focus opens up to discuss a number of wider considerations to create the conditions and atmosphere that facilitates an idea orientated workplace.

Chapter 7   IMS for Creativity & Innovation

This chapter is intended as a general introductory overview, not an exhaustive voyage into the vast field that encompasses creativity and innovation.

The Why?

"Imagine if 1 percent of the ideas, improvements, and solutions swimming in the minds of our workers were acknowledged, considered, and implemented. Our world would change in remarkable ways, and America would gain a huge economic advantage." Craig Ross (Pathways to Leadership Inc.)

Innovation is ranked as one of the top three corporate initiatives in over 70% of Fortune 500 companies.

- Innovation means Advancement
- Innovation means Survival
- Innovation means Competitiveness
- Innovation means Personal Satisfaction and Employee Engagement

For most of human history privileged circumstances came from a nation's wealth of natural resources like climate, fertile soil, and natural materials. Creativity and innovation – the ability to come up with and implement a new idea is fast becoming a nation's most priceless resource.

The field of Lean and Continuous Improvement is at the heart of competitiveness. However, to thrive we now need to combine them with an innovative culture where people at all levels come forth with creative ideas and innovations. The West cannot compete on the basis of who can pay the least per hour, nor should it. We don't have a choice about becoming more creative. The return on innovation can be very much greater than any savings achieved through cost cutting.

"Creativity is more powerful than knowledge." Einstein

"The problems that exist in the world today cannot be solved by the level of thinking that created them." Einstein

The combined fields of creativity and innovation have brought us the most important progressions in our society, yet most people have not been taught how to create. The average business executive has spent 1,000 and 10,000 hours formally studying subjects such as maths, languages, and economics, but has spent less than 10 hours studying creative thinking.

A Creative Work Space

Workplace design reflects the organisation's mission and values, including the value of creativity more than any mission statement. Physical surroundings communicate unspoken

Section Four

management attitudes towards creativity in a subtle way. Reception areas are like people's homes. They tell us a lot about the culture and values of the organisation. They help inspire pride in the accomplishments achieved. What does your entrance say about your culture?

The right kind of physical work environment nurtures the creative process. Space for divergent idea generation, for incubation and thinking, and for convergence are necessary. Creativity thrives when people feel that they are in control, when they have the ability to move from a distracted workspace to a more reflective one, and where they can personalise their "incubation" spaces. Common relaxation and fun areas promote creativity; this can include pool rooms kitted out with prototypes, juke boxes, bean bags, flip charts, and stimulating wall murals. The possibility of that magical "aha" is enhanced when products are seen in their work surroundings.

It is useful to understand the benefits that colour can have on creativity: for example blue can promote calm and concentrative thinking, a red room is good to stimulate idea generation, plain blue and green are conducive to reflective thinking.

Spaces which merge the indoors with nature to boost spirits can inspire - for example flowers and plants in the office. Research has shown that this can help to produce 15% more ideas in the workplace (Ulrich 2004).

Workspaces should be designed to foster informal communication and to ensure that work visibility is high. Cross-pollination is encouraged by creating physical layouts that allow, or even force, people to interact with one another. Space for accidental or impromptu meetings between people from disparate groups can help. Office layout should support unplanned communications (coffee docks, major areas of footfall, staircases, alcoves, etc). Allow people the flexibility and control to modify the areas to fit their specific needs at any point in time. Hence it is helpful to have moveable equipment on casters or wheels. We need to design the composition and diversity of groups carefully and the places where they meet. Research has shown that the probability of people interaction is virtually zero over a distance greater than 25 metres.

The design of a new cell should foster an outpouring of creative ideas. Siemens, Congleton UK is a case in point. There, workcells are designed in an iterative way, allowing maximum participation and creativity. First, the data relating to the cell is collected by managers and engineers. This includes the expected work rates, available space, and flow arrangements such as pull with other areas. Then, a kaizen event is held that includes representation from every group concerned with the cell – operators, first line managers, engineers, purchasing, and sometimes even suppliers. The team designs the cell during the first two days. By the third day, a full scale cardboard mock-up is in place allowing experimentation through several PDSA (Plan, Do, Study, Act) cycles. Ideas arise and adjustments are made. After the event concludes, wooden or 'Crayform' workspaces are set up. But, at this stage, everything is on wheels. Over the next few weeks further adjustments are made, until the operators feel comfortable with the new design. Only then are the final steel workbenches and shelves set up.

Design the Workspace for Play!

"I never did a day's work in my life. It was all fun." Thomas Edison

Design the work space to resemble a play space as fun and enjoyment are key determinants of a creative workplace. Items such as "The Far Side" calendar and Lego®

(for quick and rough prototyping) and toys (encourage childlike behaviour and fun) are good stimuli for breeding creativity. Leave adequate wall space for white sketch boards, maps, pictures, and other engaging visuals in team breakout areas. Foster an abundance mentality with lots of diverse thinking stimulants. Infuse the surroundings with items that encourage the people to think differently about the issue or situation they face. Stock the areas with an oversupply of innovation stimuli: prototyping kits, "Post-Its" of every size and colour, masking tape, markers for drawing, modelling clay, foam, X-Acto knives, and so on. Classical music has long been associated with stimulating the right brain and creativity, and can be played in the background during creative breakout sessions etc. Some wonderful tracks to include in your creative music portfolio include:

Beethoven: Sonota No. 14 in C-Sharp Minor, Op. 27
Brahms: Concerto in a Minor, Op. 102
Chopin: Piano Concerto No. 1 in E Minor, Op. 27
Vivaldi: L'Estro Armonico, Op. 2; Concerto No. 5 in A Major

Creative Workspace @ IDEO

IDEO is consistently on the *Business Week* List of the World's Most Innovative Companies. Its studios are laid out so that everyone sees and hears everyone else's design problems, making it possible for engineers working on other projects to overhear conversations, realising they can help, and offer ideas. Gathering information from a plethora of sources also helps generate diversity in thinking and solutions. IDEO reportedly subscribes to more than 100 magazines of various kinds. There are "clubhouses" in the offices. Not strictly space per se, clubhouses are the play times of teams and departments where they can engage in non-work activities like going to a movie or a ball-game. IDEO blends talent, discipline, and fun in its own unique way. IDEO considers its office space architecture to be one of its greatest assets (adapted from Kelley and Littman 2001).

IDEO have made a discipline of amassing junk. Their offices in various locations have duplicate cabinets known as Tech boxes filled with hundreds of materials and products: tiny batteries, switches, glow-in-the dark fabric, whacky toys, flexible circuit boards, electric motors, elegant mechanisms etc. Each Tech box is maintained by a local curator and each piece is documented on IDEO's intranet. Employees can find out what each product or material is and who knows most about it inside and outside IDEO. Weekly conference calls are held with the local curators at which they talk about new entries and the uses to which items are being put to in new projects. It allows IDEO to archive its wide array of experience gained from work across many industries and share it across all studios and hence form a worldwide network. IDEO employees are constantly on the lookout for likely contenders for addition to the Tech box. Designers and engineers can fumble through the compartments, play with the items, and apply materials used by other designers and engineers within the company to their current project. The Tech Box is a valuable resource that employees use to gain stimulation, break out of fixed thinking, or simply prevent reinventing the wheel.

Creative Workplaces Play to our Senses

Divergent thinking is enhanced by the stimuli we surround ourselves with. It's particularly enhanced through stimulation of the senses. We have five senses. But we generally only use two of these in our work environment - sight and sound. So different stimuli can be introduced into the work environment. The smell of baking bread (associated with home, comfort, and pleasure), coffee (break time and socialising) or grass (childhood, summer, sporting occasions) are some familiar smells that generate positive memories. Stimuli can be designed to be appropriate to the stage of the creative process we are in, be that preparation, incubation, illumination or execution (more about these later). Pump smells through the air conditioning for the various stages of creativity, citrus to refresh, then fragrances to promote concentration, with a finish of pine forest for relaxation.

Personal Preferences

If you asked; "Where do you do get your best ideas?" The answers are varied except for one theme. Seldom does anyone say, "at work" or "sitting at the desk." The reply is more likely to be, "driving to work", "fishing", "at the coffee shop", "walking in nature", or "in the shower". So get up and go somewhere else. Or renovate the place in which you're thinking. Employees learn and think better in physical environments that suits their personal preferences. Much research shows that the environment can stimulate creativity. Certainly the opposite case is also true, that physical environments can stifle creativity as well. You need only look at your own personal experience about the places where you can't function because of noise, light, distractions, discomfort, not well equipped, phone distractions and so forth. Take a look at the following physical dimensions to see which ones describe your ideal environment:

- Management (want present or not present)
- Mobility (prefer movement or not)
- Time of day (early morning person or a night owl)
- Seating configuration (swivel chair, bean bag, bed, floor)
- Stimulus (toys, plants, paintings, windows, sculpture, other people)
- Light (natural, artificial, bright, dim, direct, indirect)
- Temperature (heaters, air conditioner, sweaters, shorts)
- Buzz (factory floor, coffee shop, busy street, retail environment, tranquil park, conversations)
- Food (coffee, water, tea, sweets)
- Organised or cluttered environment (lots of piles or a clean desk)
- Noise (silence, classical music, nature music)
- Materials (paper, laptop, note pad, canvas, clay, flip chart, modelling clay)

By building a creative workspace organisations will not only achieve the ability to be creative and innovative, but also become more attractive places to work.

Defining Creativity

Creativity is what happens when novel ideas first come to light. It can be artistic or intellectual inventiveness. Innovation is the action. Innovation involves the whole process from opportunity identification, invention through to development, prototyping, production, marketing, and sales.

Creativity can manifest in many forms. It can be technical creativity, resulting in inventions or new products. It can be artistic or musical, resulting in stunning sculptures or beautiful songs. It can be creative writing, resulting in fiction and poetry. Creativity can also be crafts you make with your hands. Being creative is seeing the same thing as everybody else but thinking of something different.

Creativity is an attitude as much as a process with various stages. A creative attitude includes the following characteristics:

- Continually looking for new aspirations, something new to realise
- General inquisitiveness and curiosity and asking "What if?"
- Enjoying the buzz from trying something different
- Taking pleasure from teaching someone a new proficiency
- A passion for solving problems
- Passion for the purpose and are persistent in your efforts to succeed

Stages of the Creative Process

Teresa Amabile has divided the creative process into four stages.

Stage 1 - Preparation is the phase where the creative person or team immerses themselves in the problem. The creative process can be stop – go at this stage due to having no sign of visible progress, but all the time the building blocks are being put in place one by one.

Stage 2 - Incubation: This is the stage where the original problem is left to simmer in the mind and the individual or team either relaxes doing something completely different or works on a different problem. The most powerful part of us, our subconscious mind continues to process the issue and suddenly ideas may be preparing to pop up whilst relaxing or in the shower etc. The challenge today lies in getting the time to think. The number one challenge is that there is a battle for mind space in today's workplace and personal environments – emails, briefs, meetings, voicemails, and face to face time, continually bombard us. We don't have time to think, we live in an age of continuous partial attention.

Stage 3 - Illumination: This refers to the moment when everything just clicks and it all gels together (usually after a sustained period of being immersed in the issue) – the magical "aha!" or "eureka!" experience. You or the group may well end up exclaiming "Why didn't we think of that before!" It is often obvious in hindsight.

Stage 4 - Execution: This is the moment the creative process ends and the innovation process begins (i.e. action). Since the execution stage is more about social knack than it is about the technical skill that produces the innovative idea, this is the stage where management can assist and remove roadblocks.

Creative Contradictions

The domain of creativity also is complex and throws up a number of paradoxes. Creativity calls both for high preparation and specific subject matter expertise as well as the fresh perspective of "wild cards". There is a need for a variety of deep knowledge specific to the task on hand from which to generate creative abrasion. Individuals who ask silly questions are vital also to break experts out of their mental ruts.

"In the beginner's mind there are many possibilities, in the experts mind there are few"
Shunryu Suzuki

Diverse groups may be good but the challenge lies in developing team cohesiveness. Empowered freedom is needed to operate creatively but so too is alignment with the organisation's strategy. Sometimes, paradoxically, waste should be encouraged in the creative process. Generate lots of ideas at the outset in terms of quantity to breed quality. The outset is the least inexpensive stage to get all the ideas out on the table, as cost rockets for rework loops back to earlier designs.

The following table list some common illusions and realities about creativity.

Illusion	Reality
"Eureka" moment	Comes from immersion in the area
Immediate brilliant idea	Many failures along the way
Individually conceived	Collaborative approach
Brand new knowledge	Built on existing knowledge
Invention	Mostly development
Original	Borrowed combinations of ideas
Look to the future	Look to past and present and enhance
Internal R & D	Input from suppliers & customers
Product pipeline in reserve	Customers input to product pipeline
Learning environment	Unlearning is just as important
Risk aversion	Embrace risk
Minimize uncertainty	Stomach uncertainty
Obedience	Challenge status quo
Control	Autonomy and trust
Conformity	Diversity
Routine and standardisation	Cross pollination into unrelated fields
Productivity & efficiency	Incorporate failure for learning
Rigid Structure & boundaries	Porous boundaries
Hierarchy	Non-hierarchical relationships

It is not necessary to know everything about your industry in order to be creative. Csikszentmihalyi (1997) stated that a certain base level of expertise in a given industry gives you the platform for expanding beyond mere proficiency into creativity. Beyond that minimum level, sometimes too much familiarity can impede with reclassifying the problem in new and innovative ways. If you don't know too much, you won't realise that it can't be done. Hence in the novice's mind there are a whole host of options, while in the experts mind there are few.

Teresa Amabile (1998) defines three components of creativity: expertise, creative-thinking skills, and motivation. The level of creative competence is dependent on the mixture of these three factors. Expertise refers to the technical and academic knowledge that that a person has related to the target field as well as their competence of knowledge management within an organisation. Creative thinking ability refers to the person's skills in the creativity process and tools that assist inventive problem solving and ideation. Motivation refers to the intrinsic and extrinsic factors driving the person. The factors are interconnected and an increase in one area has a strong positive correlation on the others. The work environment can also play a key part in increasing expertise, creative thinking, and motivation within an organisation and hence affect the creative output.

Majaro (1991) asserts that creativity can be divided into three categories, depending on how it originates. These are normative creativity, exploratory creativity and creativity by serendipity.

Normative creativity

Normative creativity centres on generating ideas to solve predefined requirements, issues and goals. A well defined scope enables this type of creativity to be less wasteful; however it can potentially place boundaries on real blue sky thinking. This type of creativity is common in organisations for solving problems and enhancing existing products and services.

Exploratory creativity

Exploratory creativity gives rise to a large array of ideas with little or no boundaries and may have little relationship to the task at hand at the time. It may cross pollinate into other industries far afield from the one being worked on. It looks for connections or similar concepts in other industries that may give the unexpected solution to the issue. It can be used in conjunction with normative creativity to provide both focus and a wider field of vision.

Creativity by serendipity

"Serendipity is looking in a haystack for a needle and discovering a farmer's daughter." Julius Comroe Jr.

The cliché that luck is when preparation meets opportunity is sometimes applied here. Many believe that the discovery does not occur by chance, but that ideas only occur "magically" to those who are intensely curious and working hard at their task in search for a break, possibilities, solutions, or inventions. Many famous inventions throughout history have been so called "accidents". Art Fry came up with the idea of Post-it® notes whilst singing in his church choir. His bookmark kept falling out. Using 3M's policy known as "bootlegging" he used some of his working hours to develop a solution to this bug problem. Indeed the low adhesive glue found on Post-it® notes was a high tack glue formulation "gone wrong". The story of the discovery of hook and loop fasteners begun with George de Mestral taking a walk through the countryside. The Swiss engineer enjoyed hunting. One morning in 1941, while returning from the fields with his dog, he noticed how difficult it was to detach the flowers of the mountain thistle from his trousers and his dog's fur. The idea for Velcro was serendipitously born, an idea that now generates revenue in the region of $200 million annually!

Drucker (1985) agrees with the above creativity types and adds a few more sources from which innovative opportunity arises from (a) unexpected occurrences (serendipity), (b) unrelated items that are connected (exploratory) (c) process needs (normative), (d) market changes (e) changes in demographics, (f) perception shifts and (g) new knowledge arrival.

Our Creative Brain

The human brain can be seen as being composed of the left and right brain; the left brain is associated with logic, detailed facts and words where as the right brain is linked with intuition, feelings, imagination, pictures, and images. In relation to creativity, there is a need to focus a persons training and education relative to the development of both sides of the brain, thus achieving a satisfactory balance within the individual.

Section Four

In addition to the two sides of the brain, you also possess a barrier device or filter, located at the base of your brain called a Reticular Activating System or RAS. This helps decide what you're aware of, and screens out redundant information, allowing only vital input into your awareness. This is why it so important to prime your mind with your creative goals and desires. Think about a time when you wanted something new, for example a new red car of a particular brand, all of a sudden you started to become aware of that particular car in your day to day life and noticed it turning up wherever you went! Take a look at this paragraph from a Cambridge University spelling study. Can you read what it says? All the letters have been mixed up. Only the first and last letter of each word is in the right place:

I cnduo't bvleiee taht I culod aulaclty uesdtannrd waht I was rdnaieg. Unisg the icndeblire pweor of the hmuan mnid, aocdcrnig to rseecrah at Cmabrigde Uinervtisy, it dseno't mttaer in waht oderr the lteerts in a wrod are, the olny irpoamtnt tihng is taht the frsit and lsat ltteer be in the rhgit pclae. The rset can be a taotl mses and you can sitll raed it whoutit a pboerlm. Tihs is bucseae the huamn mnid deos not raed ervey ltteer by istlef, but the wrod as a wlohe. Aaznmig, huh? Yaeh and I awlyas tghhuot slelinpg was ipmorantt! See if yuor fdreins can raed tihs too.

Ask yourself, does any area of my life have so many holes that I am not seeing? Maybe the acres of diamonds are right in front of you. What opportunities are we oblivious to or just filter out? Frequently, brilliant ideas, innovations, and phenomenal creations are the product of an aware person rather than a highly intelligent one. Potential perspectives are never exhausted; it's a matter of being alert.

Likewise if you keep your mind open to new ideas, your Reticular Activating System will allow necessary information to get through to your consciousness, giving you a whole world of possibilities and inspiration. Einstein, when faced with a problem, would walk away for a few minutes, and play his violin. Upon returning to the original idea, he'd often find a solution to the problem. Leaving the predicament for a while, taking a walk, or listening to music, often helps considerably in relaxing your mind, so it can solve the problem. This is the subconscious coming to the fore again and assisting in problem solving. The brain processes information every second, of every minute, of every hour, of every day. It can process half a million possibilities in a few seconds. No wonder creativity can be so easy for humans. All we have to do is learn to trust our marvellous brains and our subconscious and of course practice. That will keep the ideas flowing! And what's more we operate at less than 10% of our brains potential capacity 90% of the time, so let's get creative, your brain is like a sleeping colossus; we've massive reserves of capacity!

Everyone is born Creative

We have creative abilities that often show up very early in life. We are all born highly creative. School, society, and the expectations to conform and follow the rules numbs us of our natural innate curious and inquisitive state. Studies have shown that between the ages of three and five 98% of children register as highly creative, and this diminishes all the way through our childhood to the extent that by the time we are in our mid twenties only 2% of us register as highly creative. The good news however is that with awareness and practice we can rebuild those creative muscles and return to our inquisitive childish days, as creativity is very much a skill we can relearn.

> *"Everyone is born a genius. Society & our educational system degeniuses them."*
> Buckminster Fuller

Most importantly, you must face any creative risk with the mind of a child. Childlike creativity should be studied and emulated. Just a few minutes a day of the "no purpose" play will make a world of difference in your creativity, problem solving, mediating, teaching, or anything else that you do.

Flow in a Creative Context

The famous creativity psychologist Mihaly Csikszentmihalyi originated the term "flow" that refers to that perfect creative state. What you're doing seems unified and almost feels effortless. You feel as if you could do it in your sleep. When you're in that state of "flow", you lose all sense of time, or self-consciousness. You become so absorbed in what you're doing, you actually become lost in the activity. He describes flow as that perfect balance between challenge (assignment complexity) and ability (the person's competence level). This means that if a task is considerably outside your ability, you will undergo anxiety. If the task is well inside your capability but produces little challenge you'll become uninterested. If the job is a challenge to your skills and you're interested in overcoming that challenge, you are on road to experiencing flow. Csikszentmihalyi says, "You can't make flow happen. All you can do is learn to remove obstacles in its way." Trying too hard is one of the obstacles to the attainment of flow. When you've recognised what flow is and what it feels like, you can start to give awareness to how you got there and increase your capacity to turn it on. This state manifests the great creative energy to which you have access. Nothing is more revitalising than being "in the zone", or the "flow". Flow is always a buoyant experience and some people even refer to it as "optimal experience". Flow doesn't just happen for traditional creative types - athletes call it being "in the zone". Professionals and others also experience flow when they're completely focused on doing the thing they love.

The experience of flow is a little different for everyone but can include the following states:

- A sense of elation – of being outside of everyday reality
- Distortion in the experience of time – what you have been engrossed in for hours seems like minutes. Einstein captured this experience in the quote, "An hour sitting with a pretty girl on a park bench seems like a minute, but a minute sitting on a hot stove seems like an hour"
- A feeling of calm proficiency or enhanced creativity
- A sense of spiritual unity
- Another magical experience (sports players often report experiencing the game slowing down at the precise peak moment and the target or goal posts getting larger)
- Intrinsic motivation – whatever pursuit produces flow becomes its own reward.

Try and recognise the things that bring about the experiences described above and think about what it was about them that engrossed you so much. Try and incorporate more of those conditions into you daily life and creative work, that way you'll learn how to enhance the experience of flow in your life. Maybe it's a quiet time to yourself listening to classical music, walking in nature, doing repetitive tasks like running on a treadmill, or watching your favourite film, or simply having fun. These are the opportunities for that magical "aha" moment that may be waiting to pop to the surface. After you've enjoyed those flow moments, reflect about how it felt and how you got there. This will help further strengthen the connections for flow in your brain and increase the likelihood of re-experiencing this virtual state of ecstasy in the future.

According to Hooker & Csikszentmihalyi (2003) there are six conditions in a workplace that produce flow and creativity.

- The organisation has to value excellence – its primary aim must be to commit to doing an exceptional job in the long term, even if this hurts the short term results. This translates into providing a nurturing environment, where mistakes are endured even welcomed to instil learning.
- Vivid goals have to be communicated to the whole organisation. This means there has to be a vision where the organisation is going and the mission, i.e. how the organisation aims to get there and what its purpose is. Whilst goals should be clearly defined, the employees need to have a certain amount of autonomy on how to translate them into their work areas on daily basis.
- Real time performance feedback or close after it is significant.
- The work being performed should match people's skills otherwise individuals either get bored when overqualified or stressed when the task is too demanding. The management should seek to provide opportunities to employees that match their skill sets.
- The work environment should enable employees to focus on the task at hand. This calls for a reduction of physical and psychological distractions.
- Organisations should provide their employees with autonomy and a feeling of control.

Defining Innovation

There are at least three Levels of Innovation:

1. Incremental Innovation (Lean)

This innovation is unlikely to produce a dramatic change in business performance overnight. However sustained innovation in this area is required to fuel continuous improvement in both product and process related aspects of a business. This is required to prevent a company falling behind and enables long term survival. Indeed it is the snowball effect of incremental innovation that gives the organisation its strength and enduring power over the longer term.

2. Substantial Innovation

The type of innovation refers to the creation of business opportunities that are likely to lead the industry and are new and distinctly better than the competitor's current offering.

3. Radical Innovation

This type of innovation can turn a business on its head, creating new bases of performance, new competitors and new business models. Radical innovation frequently comes from outside an industry and is often technology related (Baker 2002).

Creativity is the conception. Innovation is the means by which creativity is nurtured to reality. It is the process of translating useful and valuable ideas into tangible outcomes of economic value through implemented actions.

Some quotations that classify innovative thinking:

Innovation is this amazing intersection between someone's imagination and the reality in which they live. Ron Johnson

Creativity is thinking up new things. Innovation is doing new things. Theodore Levitt

Nothing is original; we're all working with the same set of elements and pieces. It's the combination that creates the remarkable.
Seth Godin, The Purple Cow

Most organisations are more interested in best practice rather than different practice; hence the world is beginning to look the same. Innovation is not about best practice, it's about fresh practice.

Developing a Creative and Innovative Culture

A company's culture is composed of its formal and informal make up, and its social environment. The culture of your organisation is created by the philosophy, vision, values, beliefs, recognition systems, behaviours, and goals of your leadership team, and to a large extent, the CEO. Simply put, it is the way we do things on a day to day basis.

Sustaining an innovative culture requires companies to create environments where creative thinking is central to corporate values, actions, and assumptions. Although culture cannot be implemented, as people have to form these shared meanings themselves, it can be shaped by following certain guidelines, and by establishing surroundings, that facilitate the desired performance.

Activities to Foster a Sustainable Culture of Creativity and Innovation

"Companies are actually living organisms, not machines. We keep bringing in mechanics, when what we need are gardeners." Peter Senge

Building a culture of creativity and innovation can be perhaps best summed up by analogy to the gardener. Growing a garden takes sustained hard work and takes time to take root. It needs to be cultivated with care and the harvest doesn't come overnight. You must guard against goats, as a few of them can undo the work of many gardeners! Much of the same can be said to consciously creating a culture of creativity and innovation. It needs nurturing and lots of hard work, and whilst it won't happen overnight the results of the harvest can be great. The following paragraphs detail some activities that can help to cultivate and fertilise the ground to lay the foundations for a good harvest.

Section Four

Align with Business Needs & Perform a Baseline Measure

Clarify the organisation's strategic business objectives. Make it clear why the current state of play is no longer acceptable and that a shift towards a culture of creativity and innovation is necessary. Frame this new culture not as an initiative but as the way of doing business for the future.

> *"The greater danger for most of us lies not in setting our aim too high and falling short; but in setting our aim too low, and achieving our mark." Michelangelo*

Conduct a creative and innovative culture assessment workshop (see Appendix IV) to identify gaps and opportunities. Determine what attitudes, behaviours, beliefs, values, and most importantly actions will close this gap. Identify required innovation capabilities within the organisation for the future and decide strategies and tools to bridge the gap. Complement this sub-strategy with other change initiatives in the company and ensure strategic alignment. Form a cross functional strategic management team representative of all stakeholders accountable for driving the above gap strategy. The CEO or similar heavy hitter should sponsor the initiative and convey the vision and lead the culture change.

Engage Leadership & Build Structure:

Form a Creativity and Innovation Steering Committee with a team selected by the CEO to include senior leaders and a lead change agent. Involve as many people as you can in the development of the innovation strategy so you build alliances early. This is the "go-slow now so you go-fast later" approach. Include sceptical employees on the team as well as supporters. The role of the steering committee is to lead the implementation of the strategy and provide guidance, design the innovation process flow to be followed, review progress and metrics, and remove roadblocks etc. Communication and promotion of the change effort are also crucial. Program managers can be assigned at the value stream or business unit level to oversee and be accountable for implementation. They develop the vision and roadmap for their value streams including detail on the background and necessity for striving towards a culture of creativity and innovation. They also demonstrate the guiding principles (authenticity, respect, etc) that will become engrained in the way business is conducted going forward. They should lead by example demonstrating the values of teamwork, personal responsibility, excellence, learning form mistakes, etc. They are responsible for scoping of the initiative, timeframe, and budgeting, etc. Leadership is called for at all levels (from the front line's idea champions through to the CEO) by visionary, animated champions of change. Leaders must communicate and reinforce the newly defined core values, beliefs, and norms of creative culture. They also serve as role models to the employees who look to them to provide inspiration, support for their ideas, and leadership. Top management support and encouragement of creativity, both financial and psychological are vital.

Give every staff member clear roles and responsibilities to build their sense of ownership and align their focus to working towards the company vision. The IMS should be marketed as the mechanism to capture employee's nuggets of wisdom and be the wellspring for creativity. Manage as though we expect creativity from everyone -- not just isolated "solitary geniuses" (adapted from the work of O' Donovan 2003).

Make Innovation a Process & Provide Resources:

The cycle of implementing creative product ideas and capturing employee's ideas should be designed as a repeatable process. Every other critical business goal is supported by a defined process. A defined process enables innovation to be repeatable and sustainable. The innovation process includes the end to end process from trend spotting, to understanding customer needs, to commercialising an idea, and launching it as a new product or service. It also incorporates the company's IMS system for incremental improvements. Develop staff roles to support the process at various stages (adapted from Philips 2008).

A budget should be assigned to support the innovation process. Pilot 'ideation' events supported by trained event facilitators can be run at the outset to demonstrate the concept and power of innovation. Changes and ideas can then be passed on to the entire workplace and become embedded as the way we work from now on. This allows the shift away from event type ideation towards becoming a part of the natural daily work culture.

Measure the Process:

Create a family of metrics in conjunction with all key stakeholders that support the organisation's innovation strategy, a selection that is congruent for the organisation's needs should be selected across the three categories below:

Input Metrics
- Resources allocated to innovation – people, time, and budget
- % of employees trained in the tools of creativity
- % of executives time spent on strategic innovation versus day-today operations
- numbers of ideas generated

Process Metrics
- Average time from idea approval to implementation
- Number of ideas approved and number implemented
- League tables of ideas implemented by area
- Value of the innovation pipeline in terms of new product potential and cost avoidance

Output Metrics
- Number of new products or services launched
- $ savings from internally implemented ideas
- Revenue from new products or services
- ROI on innovation budget
- Number of new customers
- Relativity metric (comparison metric to similar external organisations)

A structured activity of monitoring metrics against goals as a means to gauge progress is recommended. Innovative leaders manage by asking searching questions and encourage open constructive critique not cynical dissent.

Section Four

Spread the Word:

Employees should be encouraged to borrow ideas with pride both from within the company and externally. Somebody else has definitely solved our specific problem concept before, so go find out where! Establish a Creativity & Innovation Library and stock it with an array of creativity books, DVD's, podcasts etc. on the topic. Perhaps hold a series of lunch discussion groups or book clubs with live Q & A sessions on a particular topic.

Loosen Controls:

The organisation's recruitment practices, its methods of assigning responsibilities, the way groups within the organisation interact, and the way achievements in the company are celebrated and recognised needs to be reviewed in terms of promoting creativity. Creating a true feeling of empowerment among employees is central to fostering a culture of innovation. Assigning ownership of activities and giving employees the authority to make appropriate decisions are significant motivational tactics. Companies can empower their employees by encouraging divergent thinking, listening to them and being open to new ideas, and ensuring that they have the information and resources they need to follow through with their ideas. Empowerment does not mean simply handing over control. Freedom and authority must be complemented with accountability, management discipline, and feedback. Also, a consensus on the qualitative and quantitative metrics that will govern success must be created. Indeed people must be given sufficient time to pursue creative activities, some slack time should be designed into their roles and responsibilities for this propose. Google and 3M, two of the world's most consistently innovative organisations, allow their employees in the region of 10-20% of their work week as slack time to work on their passionate and creative projects. Along with designing slack time into people's roles, incubation time should also be considered to allow adequate time for ideas to develop and mature. Innovative organisations recognise that ideas need to gestate in the subconscious mind where they mature. This process takes time and requires an element of freedom. You need a culture where people have the autonomy to explore, share, and develop ideas and the authority to progress those ideas into practice.

Endorse Fun:

Play relaxes people and opens their minds to new possibilities, and helps them make connections that improve the quality of their thinking. Give your work group opportunities to master their play skills. The key to letting people have room to "play" is to refrain from judgment of their seemingly irrelevant activities or methods.

Develop People:

Create an innovation centre in your organisation where tools and resources help individuals to practise new ways of thinking. The creativity and innovation library could also be located here. Instead of seeing creativity education as a way to pour knowledge into people's heads, see it as a way to polish new lenses for people so they can see the world in a different way.

Teach, hold classes, and mentor people in the use of creativity and lateral thinking tools to facilitate creative thinking. People have become programmed to think in a certain way and tools are required to wrench people out of their predefined patterns and unchanged thinking. Research has determined that people have 60,000 thoughts a day, and that 57,000 of them are the same as the day before! It's incredible when you think about how unconscious we really are, hence the need for tools.

"When The Student Is Ready, The Teacher Shall Appear"
Chinese Proverb

Appreciate the Long Term Perspective:

There is an innate tendency for managers to pull out "saplings" to see how well the roots are "growing". Impatience and pressure for immediate results are among the usual suspects. Resist this temptation to look for immediate results. When building a culture that truly encourages innovation, the pressure to get immediate results will yield only short burst improvements, and the need to meet deadlines can sometimes kill the creative process before the illumination stage. While it is true that deadlines can focus creative teams and encourage timely resolution, setting deadlines should not be overused because they often will interfere with the creative process. Close communication with creative people working on a project can help leaders develop a feel for when setting a deadline will help, rather than hinder the process (adapted from Dundon 2002).

Communicate & Involve Everyone:

Encourage active communication. Innovation requires communication. Sharing thoughts multiples the opportunities for unique insights and powerful ideas. Communication also creates an environment of mutual support among co-workers. Set up communication forums. A robust communication system ensures that all employees are aligned to the company's vision and are clear that they are empowered to be creative and unconventional in their thinking and approach to work. This is however in alignment with achieving a focused overall objective.

A creative culture places emphasis on how vital it is to channel and leverage all the talent of the full organisation; the Idea Management System is an excellent vehicle for this. The subtle message is that we want the input of all people who work here; we are equal and no hierarchy exists.

Build motivation to use people's creative talents and market them as a life skill; especially appeal to people's internal intrinsic motivation.

"Don't ask yourself what the world needs; ask yourself what makes you come alive. And then go and do that. Because what the world needs are people who have come alive." Harold Whitman

Embrace Learning:

Leaders must maximise opportunities to learn. Help people gain the courage to act by serving as a cushion and finding ways to absorb risk. Stress the importance of learning from mistakes (view them as experiments, then they are not failures!) and follow through by looking for those learning opportunities. Show people that you support their attempts to innovate by your attitude. Give their half baked ideas a chance, and recognise innovation when it happens. Providing a wide variety of opportunities for learning, organisations expose their employees to a greater variety of stimuli, enhance their motivation to learn new things, and create the knowledge and skills for them to develop and work with new innovations.

"Failure is simply the opportunity to begin again, this time more intelligently."
Henry Ford

Generate Ideas:

Organise planned brainstorming sessions on strategic issues and have them open to all employees. During these sessions, ensure that all ideas are heard and fairly evaluated.

Enrich People's Jobs:

There are a number of things you can do to enrich people's jobs including increasing skill variety, giving them more autonomy, providing ongoing feedback. Redesign work to allow employees to perform a complete, integrated piece of work, and give them information on how what they do impacts customers and the organisation, so they can better understand the benefits of their work. Allow job rotation. For example, have a manufacturing engineer spend time in the field with your sales team to observe direct customer experience. Implement a mentorship program with senior personnel and new employees to immerse them in the culture that is been formulated. Use the perspective of new employee's fresh eyes also to garner insight into opportunities and overcome "workplace blindness". New employees really are a great source of new ideas. Get new hires together and tap their brainpower and imagination. Create cross-functional teams to complete creative projects that are of strategic importance. In each team, include individuals from different groups, geographical locations, and, if possible, cultural backgrounds. Establish an Innovation Centre of Excellence in your business complete with idea "war" rooms and "skunk works" facilities. Create a regular schedule of mini-conferences where internal groups present their ideas to one another. This captures and communicates innovation best practices and inspires further creative work. Use events, such as sporting activities, charity events, or lunchtime lectures to promote inter-departmental interaction. Organise an annual creativity and innovation week where people can showcase their creative work.

Nurture Innovation Activity:

To build an innovative hub in a business for accelerated creative work, management may want to select the most capable creative personalities and nurture them with extra resources. Make it clear to other employees in advance what the purpose of such activity is. However this concentrated hub should not be viewed as a substitute for the development of a pervasive creative culture across the organisation. Leaders should train other managers to understand the stages of the creative process (preparation, incubation, illumination, and execution), and evaluate managers based on their ability to promote and steer through to completion new ideas from their team. Encourage a mindset which drives thinking of everything as an "experience". Think about all the activities that a user would go through when using the product or service and try to design the perfect stress free and absorbing experience. On a similar note market the *benefits* of a new product or service rather than features such as a new add on etc.

Test & Experiment then Implement:

Both a culture of experimentation (again this implies that it's a trial and will not be viewed as a failure) and a culture of critique are called for in a creative work environment. A culture of critique means that people recognise the process of how to evaluate and receive feedback on ideas and don't become defensive. The person receiving constructive criticism has to be able to listen to everything that is said, and in turn, move it forward. A lot of organisations see critique as negative. But it is not; it should be seen as exploratory and constructive.

Commit to driving the best ideas through to implementation: innovators are seldom the best salespeople for their ideas. The leader's driving innovation must act as the first-line filter to test the best ideas and solutions, choosing which ones are the right ones to see through to fruition. One of the things that can kill creativity quicker than anything else is an over-reliance on rigid policies. In creative cultures policies and standards are viewed as the current best known way, and can, and should be, continually challenged to spark new and innovative approaches.

Manage for Creativity:

Overhaul your performance review approach to identify the key personal strengths, in terms of hard skills and mind-set that encourage creative abrasion and expression. Take the time to understand employees' career goals and aspirations and to create individual development plans for each employee. Many managers bring far too much ego and self importance to work everyday. Set it down at the door. Leaders should ask their employees, "What's the one thing I could do to make things better for you?", then listen and take appropriate action. The main part of your job is to stimulate the individual creativity of your employees and as Gary Convis, former Toyota President, elegantly stated, "The art of true management is leading as if you have no authority." Encourage people to question your decisions and logic...it will help you refine your critical thinking skills and also build that in your employees. Adults learn best when they self-discover. Rather than directing employees, use a "coach approach" to encourage self-discovery and lead by asking thought-provoking open-ended questions.

Open Innovation:

Develop an on-line submission process for gathering external customer ideas. Proctor and Gamble have used this open innovation technique with huge success to the extent that 35% of their new products are now originated from outside the company.

Become a Trend Spotter:

As an organisation, keep abreast of the latest trends in your industry and indeed outside your industry. Recent trends include, the effects and opportunities brought about by the global recession, the rise in aging population, sharp increase in single occupancy homes/single parent families, increasing awareness of sustainability/green issues, internet shopping/delivery of consumables, increasing desire to simplify a highly complex world, and a desire for more convenience doing mundane tasks. Trends are rich sources of emerging consumer needs and fertile sources for innovative opportunities.

Different Stance:

Deliberately take a different point of view; look at things from a new perspective. First Dutch Boy redesigned their paint can by making it cube shaped and providing a screw-off cap. Innovation can be elegant simplicity if we just look at things in a different way. Define what does perfect mean for your customer before solving all the "yes buts" (Philips 2008).

Understand Value:

Ensure that your staff are aware of the four categories of customer value that contribute to the price a product will demand in the marketplace. The utility, or *use value,* is the most obvious. How effective is the product at solving the customer's specific problem? In addition, many products provide *esteem value,* meaning that they somehow increase our sense of well-being. Furthermore, if a product embodies labour and/or materials that are known to be in short supply, *the scarcity* value of the product could be significant. Finally, even if the product isn't scarce, doesn't solve your particular problem, and fails to raise your self-esteem, if it holds or appreciates in value over time it therefore accrues *exchange value.* For a product to command a relatively high market price, it must embody a positive combination of all four of these value categories (adapted from Smith & Krueger 2003). Note that a change in just one of the four categories can make a substantial difference in the price of a product.

Innovation Personas

Tom Kelley in his excellent book called *The Ten Faces of Innovation* details the personas (or different perspectives) that are sought for in organisations to foster and cultivate the spirit of innovation. Adopting one or more of these roles (similar in some ways to DeBono's Six Thinking Hats, see chapter 8) can help teams convey a different point of view and create a broader range of innovative solutions. This spirit of innovation is a way of life and permeates the entire culture at great companies. Innovation leaders should try and display a piece of all "Ten Faces of Innovation". They should also identify internal innovation supporters and recognise their "Face". Innovation leaders should also know who the "Devils Advocates" are in their organisation and be prepared for them. The devil's advocates may be the biggest innovation killers in organisations today. Every day, thousands of great new ideas, concepts, and plans are nipped in the bud by overly negative killer phrases from these devil's advocates. The sort of killer phrases you hear include:

- Put it in writing
- Don't ask questions; just follow the rules
- You need the approval of many levels
- I personally wouldn't do it, but you can try
- What would the boss think?
- Don't rock the boat
- We've never done it this way before

The essence of the Ten Faces are summarised below:

People who adopt the learning roles (1-3 below) are humble enough to question their own worldview, and in doing so, they remain open to new insights. These personas are driven by the idea that no matter how successful a company currently is, no one can afford to be complacent.

1. The Cross-Pollinator creates opportunities by drawing associations and connections between unrelated ideas and concepts. They bring ideas into the organisation from the outside world.

2. The Anthropologist delivers insights into the organisation by observing human behaviour and developing a deep understanding of how people interact physically and emotionally with products, services, and work spaces. When an IDEO human-factors person camps out in a hospital room for 48 hours with an elderly patient undergoing surgery, they are living the life of the anthropologist and helping to develop new health-care services.

3.	The Experimenter prototypes new ideas quickly and continuously, learning by a process of trial and error. The Experimenter takes calculated risks to achieve success through a state of "experimentation as implementation."

The next three personas are organising and facilitating roles:

4.	The Hurdler knows that the path to innovation is strewn with obstacles and develops a knack for overcoming or outsmarting those roadblocks. When the 3M worker who invented masking tape decades ago had his idea initially rejected, he refused to give up. Staying within his $100 authorisation limit, he signed a series of $99 purchase orders to pay for critical equipment needed to produce the first batch. His perseverance paid off, and 3M has reaped billions of dollars in cumulative profits because an energetic Hurdler was willing to bend the rules.

5.	The Collaborator helps bring diverse groups together, and often leads from the middle of the pack to create new combinations and multidisciplinary solutions.

6.	The Director not only gathers together a talented cast and crew but also helps to spark their creative talents. When a creative Mattel executive assembles an ad hoc team of designers and project leaders, sequesters them for 12 weeks, and ends up with a new $100 million girls-toy platform in three months, she is a role model for Directors everywhere.

The last four faces are known as the building or nurturing personas:

7.	The Experience Architect designs compelling experiences that go beyond mere functionality to connect at a deeper level with customers' latent or unexpressed needs.

8.	The Set Designer creates a stage on which innovation team members can do their best work, transforming physical environments into powerful tools to influence behaviour and attitude. They create work environments that celebrate the individual and stimulate creativity, thereby promoting energetic, inspired cultures.The right office environments can help nourish and sustain a creative culture. Continuous innovation is enhanced by adjusting physical spaces and balancing private and collaborative work opportunities. Organisations that tap into the power of the Set Designer oftentimes discover remarkable performance improvements that make all the space changes worthwhile.

9.	The Caregiver builds on the metaphor of a health-care professional to deliver customer care in a manner that goes beyond mere service. They work to understand individual customers and create relationships through empathy. Good Caregivers anticipate customer needs and are ready to look after them. When you see a service that's really in demand, there's usually a Caregiver at the heart of it.

10.	The Storyteller builds both internal morale and external awareness through compelling narratives that communicate a fundamental human value or reinforce a specific cultural trait. Companies from Apple to Starbucks have lots of corporate legends that support their brands and build camaraderie within their teams. Medtronic, celebrated for its product innovation and consistently high growth, reinforces its culture with straight-from-the-heart storytelling - patients' firsthand narratives of how the products changed or even saved their lives.

The personas are about "being innovation" rather than merely "doing innovation." Take on one or more of these roles, and you'll be taking a conscious step toward becoming more of an innovator in your daily life (adapted from Fast Company Dec. 2007 report on Kelley & Littman 2005).

Risk Taking

A culture of creativity and innovation requires a failure tolerant culture; this means that the workplace must develop a cultural acceptance of risk taking and embracing and learning from failure. Hence risk taking and failure should not be viewed negatively. Thomas Edison failed 1000 times developing the light bulb; however he viewed them as learning opportunities. View failures as opportunities for growth. The key to success in any discipline is rapid safe failure, akin to a child learning to ride a bike and learning how to fall without hurting themselves.

Remember that people are vulnerable when they come up with a new idea at first. Make them feel less vulnerable by reducing their anxiety. Be graceful about feedback you give on your people's ideas. A non threatening culture is where there is a shared belief that a well intentioned action will not lead to punishment or rejection. One of the biggest reasons why you might not nurture your creative side is fear - fear of making a mistake. Remember that perfectionism is a deterrent to your creativity. Albert Einstein noted that "a person who's never made a mistake has never tried anything new." Don't let fear keep you from being creative. You don't learn as much from winning as you do from losing. The upside of not succeeding right away is that we often encounter the magical serendipity. So let people know that it's acceptable to experiment and try new things in the name of proactive improvement seeking.

Note: See Appendix III for 30 Ways to Increase Your Personal Creativity and Appendix IV for the Creative & Innovative Workplace Survey

Section Five

This section provides a series of twenty creativity tools that can be taught to employees to improve the authentic quality of their ideas and/or to improve general creative thinking ability. At the outset of an idea system employees will probably have vast stored reserves of ideas and will not need any stimulants to offer creative ideas. However in line with Imai's concept of the Kaizen Flag we need to spend a proportion of time on breakthrough thinking also. However the following set are extremely powerful and were used in some combination to bring us the greatest innovations that history has provided us with.

Although these tools can be used for general, unlimited creativity, they are best used in an industrial or service setting when focused on a particular aim or problem.

Chapter 8   Resources for Thinking

Chapter 5 detailed some of the problem solving tools for tackling existing issues. In this chapter we look at some creativity tools that can be used to give us new perspectives on existing issues and to come up with totally new ideas and possibilities. These tools can be likened to pulling a rabbit out of the hat!

> *"Just as energy is the basis of life itself, and ideas the source of innovation, so is innovation the vital spark of all human change, improvement and progress."*
> Theodore Levitt

The ways in which you repeatedly think becomes a habit. If you learn the techniques of creative thinking, and use them until they are a habit, then creative thinking will become a natural thing for you. In essence they enable us to escape mentally from our conditioned thinking patterns.

Tool # 1:   Bug Listing

Adams in *Conceptual Blockbusting: A Guide to Better Ideas* describes this creative technique. This is a method for identifying under-served customer needs. A bug list should spark ideas in your mind for new ideas and inventions for both products and services.

Write down things that annoy you or cause problems for you. Then think of some possible solutions for these. Develop the habit of taking notes and writing down these things on a daily basis. Carry a small notebook around with you or use your personal PDA to record those bugs you encounter in real time.

Example bugs could be;

- Difficultly opening a tomato ketchup sachet
- Neighbours house alarm going off in a hail shower
- Waiting in line for a service provider
- Wrong meal served up in a restaurant
- Carrying heavy grocery bags
- General boredom whilst travelling

Tool # 2:   Random Word

Michalka in his excellent book *Cracking Creativity* describes this technique as a way to "connect the unconnected". He states that in order to get new ideas, you need a way to produce new sets of patterns in your mind. The "random word" technique generates an almost infinite source of new patterns to react with the patterns already in your mind. They are like pebbles being dropped into a pond. They stimulate waves of associations and connections, some of which may help you to a breakthrough idea.

> *"Nothing is new except arrangement."*
> William J. Durant

Edward de Bono also favours this technique, calling it "Po Thinking". Not No, but Po. Let it swirl around in your mind for a while, and develop the connections.

Choose a word at random either from a random word list, a dictionary, a book index, flicking through the channels on your TV and writing down the first object that you are attracted to, listening to and recording nature's sounds and so forth. The important thing is that the words are random and that you don't edit them in any way; that is go with the hand that you have been dealt. You can also combine concepts. A concept is really the essence of something, for example a mobile phone is a communication device. When you've selected two words, think about the words. Get clear in your mind what each represents. In a notebook, draw a mind map (see Tool # 16 below) of each word and tease out what each means and represents to you. Some questions to ask that will help connect your random trigger word to your idea include:

- How is the problem or idea like the trigger word?
- Does the issue or opportunity have the trigger word in it?
- What are the attributes that the word associates within your memory?
- What is the word like?
- What is it not like?
- What does the word suggest?

Example:

- Challenge: How do we prevent vandalism of the local club building?
- Random Word: wine-box (selected by random flicking through a book)
- Associations for wine-box include:

  a) alcoholic drink
  b) glass
  c) label
  d) container
  e) print
  f) relax
  g) fridge
  h) red and white
  i) expensive (or cheap!)
  j) tax

Bridging ideas include:

a) Is there a trend as to when the vandalism happens, e.g. night time or at weekends when people are drinking?
b) Strong glass. But also "see through" leading to: Can they see in? (how do they see us?) Can we see out? (from their perspective)
c) Post up trespassing warnings. But also "signs", leading to "What do our signs say? What should they say?
d) What is being "boxed up"? (Are we too boxed up? Could we open the box? Pandora?)
e) Print a list of offenders caught in local papers? Cover the walls with posters (print) so that graffiti cannot be clearly seen?
f) If teenagers use the area to relax, can we provide an alternative?
g) How to "freeze out" vandals? Ban? Shame?
h) Security alarms are equipped with red and white flashing beacons
i) Trespassers are fined (Or let them in for free – make it their club.)

j) Members are incentivised to keep an eye out for vandals as membership fees will be lowered by the amount equivalent to the drop in vandalism costs

Tool # 3   Finding New Applications

This is another technique, which like word combination, can be used in all areas to create new ideas. Start with the essence of the idea, and look for new applications. Then look at any other factors that could be applied in new ways.

Example:
An ATM machine delivers cash to the customer. The essence is that it delivers paper slips in accurate amounts. Could we use ATM's to deliver parking tickets hence avoiding unsightly parking meters on the street? Or maybe to deliver cinema or bus or rail tickets?

Tool # 4:   Challenging Assumptions (adapted from Michalka 2001)

"The hardest assumption to challenge is the one you don't even know you are making."
Douglas Adams

Assumptions are really our mental maps; we believe that a situation we're facing is like other situations we've faced before, and that what worked then will do once again. The more skilled we are in a particular area, the more likely we are to bring lots of prejudice to the problem, which can inhibit us from finding original and creative solutions.
Many great new ideas are the result of people who were willing to question current assumptions and paradigms. Challenging assumptions is important for creativity because it compels us to look beyond what is already accepted or appears to be set in stone. People's assumptions of things can be embedded so deeply that it never crosses their minds to question them. They can strangle our creativity and the result is the more or less the same conditioned thinking leading to a set of imitative solutions.

- Write down your challenge and list assumptions (an accepted truth that is not challenged)
- What are the assumptions you are making about it? What seems so accepted that you would never think about challenging it?
- Challenge and/or reverse assumptions
- Ask "How or in what circumstances could this be false?"
- Find ways of making the challenge reality

This is another assumptive challenge.

Example:

Challenge: The global recession is the reason for restaurant sales decline.
Assumption: People are only buying necessities.
Break the assumption: Other food industries such as pizza takeaways are thriving in the recession.
Assumption: Home consumption is less expensive.
Break the assumption: We use the same ingredients and facility overheads.
Assumption: Our catering staff raises our costs.
Break the assumption: We can establish an in house self catering option to compete with local take away competitors.

"Discovery consists of seeing what everybody has seen and thinking what nobody has thought." Albert Szent-Gyorgyl

Tool # 5:   What-If?

Benjamin Franklin the famous statesman and inventor from the 1700's reputably used this technique to fashion some of his inventions. This method of creating ideas has one foot grounded in reality and one in a fantasy world. A central block to creativity is the mind's firm grasp on reality. The secret to this exercise is to withhold judgment and see what ideas you can come with....don't worry about practicality.

"Imagination is more important than knowledge. For while knowledge defines all we currently know and understand, imagination points to all we might yet discover and create." Albert Einstein

Method:
- Write down your challenge. "In what other ways might we...?"
- List as many "what if" scenarios as you can
- Try to answer the questions posed by your scenarios

Example:
- A)   What if I got paid $1000 for each book I have read?
- B)   What if I earned $1000 each night I slept?
- C)   What if money rained down on my house?

Answers:
- A)   Join a book review panel and publish a critique of the book in a leading magazine
- B)   Set up an internet store selling products via drop shipment (passive income stream)
- C)   It does – like rain or sun! But much goes to waste, so....install a low friction rotation electric turbine in the gutter to capture potential energy in falling rain, use to light the garden for free.

The main benefit of this exercise is to train the mind to explore fantasy as reality and to think about the logical actions needed to support such a change in real things.

Tool # 6   Attribute Listing and SCAMPER

Robert C. Crawford, of University of Nebraska who taught creativity classes in the 1950s, wrote about attribute listing in his book, *The Techniques of Creative Thinking* published in 1954 (yes 1954!). Attribute listing takes an existing product or service, breaks it into parts, identifies various ways of achieving each part, and then recombines these to identify new versions of the product or system. Descriptive attributes can include substance, structure, colour, shape, texture, sound, taste, space, odour and density.

SCAMPER is a checklist of provoking questions you might not normally ask that helps you to think of changes you can make to an existing product or service or to create a new one. The questions were earlier developed by Alex Osborn and later rearranged by Bob Eberle into SCAMPER. The questions SCAMPER stands for are detailed below and you can add and expand your own additional questions:

Substitute	Can I substitute something else? Who else? What else? Other ingredients? Other material? Other power? Other place?
Combine	What can be combined? Combine materials? What other products can be merged with this?
Adapt	What else is like this? What other ideas does this suggest? Does the past offer a solution? Whom could I copy or draw inspiration from?
Magnify/Modify	What can be magnified made larger or extended? What can be exaggerated? What can be added? More time? Stronger? Higher? Longer? How can this be altered for the better? What can be modified? Is there a new twist? Change meaning, color, motion, smell, form, shape? Change name?
Put to other use	What else could this be used for? Are there any other ways to use as is?
Eliminate	What are the opposites? What are the negatives? Should I turn it around? Up instead of down? Down instead of up?
Reverse/Rearrange	What if it were smaller? Understated? What should I omit? Delete? Subtract? What is unnecessary? Streamline? Make miniature? Condense? Compact? What other rearrangement might be better? Interchange components?

SCAMPER: Make an idea-prompting poster by printing this table and placing it in a prominent position in your workplace.

Method:
Focus on each specific attribute and try to improve it.

- State your challenge.
- Analyse the challenge and list as many attributes as you can.
- Take each attribute, one at a time, and try thinking of alternate ways to change and improve it. Use the SCAMPER checklist for each attribute.
- Combine one or more of these alternative ideas and see if you can come up with an enhanced new design for the product or service.
- Example:
- Challenge: Design a better teapot
  Attributes of a teapot
    - Aluminium Vessel
    - Round Container
    - Silver Colour
    - Metal Handle
    - Conducts heat
    - Silent (no noise)

Using the SCAMPER Questions we stimulate alternatives to the above attributes

- Have a transparent tea pot with inner suspended decorative tea bags
- Tea pot changes colour when ready, i.e. tea has drawn and is ready to pour
- The teapot is shaped as a horizontal cylinder for enhanced aesthetics

- Conical (stable, low centre of gravity) for safety on airplanes and hospitals
- Kettle & Teapot ("all in one")
- Inner pot decorations (plants, suspended teabags)
- Have an Oxo style "Gud Grips" handle for elderly
- "Cool Touch" double wall insulated body
- Cup/Toast "keep warm" heating plate on teapot lid
- It plays relaxing nature music

Combining some or all of the above attributes opens up many creative options to design a contemporary new teapot, a product not generally associated with innovation!

Tool # 7:   Morphological Analysis

Morphological Analysis was developed by Fritz Zwicky (the Swiss astrophysicist and aerospace scientist based at the California Institute of Technology) in the 1940's and 50's as a method for systematically structuring and investigating a total set of relationships. Morphological Analysis is an extension of Attribute Listing.

Imagine you have a product that could be made of six types of material, in six possible shapes, in six possible carrying mechanisms, in six colours and with six kinds of closing devices. Theoretically there are 180 (6 x 6 x 5) potential combinations of materials, shapes, carrying mechanisms, colours and closing devices. Some of these combinations may already exist; others may be ridiculous or impractical. Those left over may represent potential new product ideas.

Method:

- List the attributes of the problem, object, or situation as you would in a standard attribute analysis.
- Under each attribute, list all the alternatives you can think of.
- Choose an alternative from each column at random and assemble the choices into a possibility for a new idea. Repeat the choice and combination of attributes many times to spark new ideas.

Example:

Develop an alternate to a rucksack.

What are the current attributes of a rucksack? In the table below the attributes are listed in the first row and alternates are listed under each attribute:

Nylon	*Rectangular*	*Two straps*	*Coloured*	*Zipped*
steel	*cylindrical*	*one strap*	*transparent*	*magnetic*
plastic	*sphere*	*velcro*	*glow in dark*	*flip lid*
glass	*oval*	*helium*	*net*	*pea pod*
wooden	*triangle*	*wheels*	*invisible*	*glue*

Section Five

leather	square	floating	flashing	gravity
stone	hexagonal	hands free	trend follower	sensor

The following row of words is randomly selected to spark new associations and ideas for a rucksack (travel bag).

Leather, Cylindrical, Wheels, Glow in Dark, Sensor

Studying the above row of words for a few minutes sparks the possibility of having a cylindrical travel bag that doubles as its own wheel. The cylindrical bag with a hard outer plastic casing lies horizontally on the floor and has a telescopic handle like traditional suit cases. Integrated into the handle is a push button that powers the bag to spin. This enables the bag to self drive avoiding traveller fatigue. The bag could be florescent to enhance safety via improving its visibility.

Tool # 8   Action Words

This tool uses a list of action words (verbs) to stimulate creative thinking. You can make your own list of words too. Choose one of the verbs and think about how it can be applied to your idea or problem.

Example:

The problem is to improve machine downtime.

run	condense	spin
shower	twist	break
crush	melt	swing
flash	tighten	dip
shut	reschedule	walk

The verb is spin.

What does that suggest?

Rotate the usage of the machine by utilising back up machines and perform maintenance on one whilst the other is in use. What forces are acting on the machine and causing it to breakdown? What are the top three breakdown reasons? Are all shifts seeing the machine breaking down like this or is it isolated to one shift? Can we install sensors to detect deterioration before the machine breaks? Etc.

Tool # 9   Reversal

This was originally developed by Steve Grossman and described by Arthur VanGundy in his book, *Techniques of Structured Problem Solving*. Reversals break your existing patterns of thought and incite new ways of thinking.

Method:
- State your challenge. In what ways might I…….
- List your assumptions
- Challenge your supporting and underlying assumptions (seek someone else's perspective, reverse the obvious)
- Reverse the assumption. Write down the opposite of each one.
- Record different insights that proves useful.

Example:
- Challenge: In what ways might we save energy in the hospital?
- List our assumptions.
  - ✓ Energy costs money
  - ✓ We must turn off unused lights and equipment
  - ✓ People must be given energy awareness training
  - ✓ It is showing social responsibility to reduce our carbon footprint

- Challenge the above assumptions.
  - ✓ Energy is generated for free from nature
  - ✓ The technology exists for lights and equipment to self shut down
  - ✓ People often behave differently at home than at work
  - ✓ What if we used our energy waste to help others?

- Reverse the above assumptions.
  - ✓ Energy is free
  - ✓ Leave unused lights and equipment on continually
  - ✓ People already know how to conserve energy
  - ✓ It is socially responsible to increase our carbon footprint

- Useful perspectives from above reversals
  - ✓ Install solar panels on the hospital roof to generate free solar energy
  - ✓ Install motion sensors in rooms to turn lights out after 10 minutes of non detected activity. Install vibration sensors on non critical machines to auto turn off when not in use
  - ✓ Run a themed "Do as you would at home" week, to raise awareness about energy wastage
  - ✓ Promote a campaign stating that 10% of savings from energy reduction will be donated to the needy and hungry. This should intrinsically motivate responsible behaviour around energy usage.

Tool # 10:   Analogy or Metaphor

The analogy has been used as a creative catalyst perhaps since the beginnings of human existence. Leonardo Da Vinci's notebooks are inundated with analogies to nature. Robert Frost stated that education by poetry is education by metaphor. Indeed powerful metaphors are to be found in all enduring literature.

Section Five

Analogies or metaphors make us challenge assumptions that can lead to new insights and ideas.

"The metaphor is probably the most fertile power possessed by men."
Ortega Y Gassett

You use an analogy when you say that something is like something else (in some aspects but not in others).

- State your challenge
- Choose a key word or phrase in the challenge
- Choose a different setting, preferably a diverse area (different industry, business, department)
- Generate a list of items that you associate with this setting
- Look for similarities or connections between the above settings and your challenge. Relax don't force things.
- Do these connections give rise to any bridging ideas?

Example:

- Prevent patients falling in hospitals. 25% of patients with hip fractures die within a year and only 25% recover fully (Source: Grunden 2008).

- Falling is the key phrase in the challenge.

- Patients falling is like a **building site** (selected analogy)

- Images of a building site include lots of busy activity, multiple machine types, bricks and mortar, sand, workers wearing helmets, noise, scaffolding, fork lift trucks, clay etc.

- Similarities include:
- Hospitals are also very busy and at some periods more than others
- There are lots of machines and clutter in many hospital wards etc.
  - ✓ Hospitals floors are also made from concrete
  - ✓ Patients don't generally wear head and body protection
  - ✓ Hospital beds have noise (alarm) beepers
  - ✓ Some beds use a form of scaffolding (bed side rails)
  - ✓ Hoists are used instead of fork truck to lift immobile patients
  - ✓ Fibre glass is a form of clay used in hospitals for casting limb fractures

- Bridging ideas are:
  - ✓ Keep records of where and when patients fall. Look for trends – shift handover etc, when staff on ward is lower?
  - ✓ De-clutter our wards and improve line of sight for all patients
  - ✓ Ensure that patients in pain can reach bed alarms without having to get out of bed
  - ✓ Identify high risk fall category patients with red wrist bands and provide lower beds, padding, and bed side rails etc.
  - ✓ Provide nurse support and walking aids etc. if patients need to use toilets
  - ✓ Use children's play mats around the floor of beds for high risk fall category patients to provide padding in the unfortunate event of a fall

Tool #11   Random Objects

Michael Michalko (2001) in the chapter called "Making Novel Connections" of *Cracking Creativity*, details a wonderful tool called Random Objects. He states that combining two dissimilar subjects creates a cognitive fusion that sometimes leads to a novel insight or idea.

This tool is great for coming up with ideas for new products. Randomly select say 22 objects (real or imaginary) and list them in two columns across from each other as below. Work your way down the sheets combining all the words against each other. For example you would combine mirror – poster and also reverse the association as in poster – mirror. This could spark the idea of having a children's mirror with a cartoon poster embedded behind the mirror. Another example is cartoon – badge or badge – cartoon; this may provide the idea of having a funny cartoon caricature impression of people on their company name badges to promote workplace morale and humor.

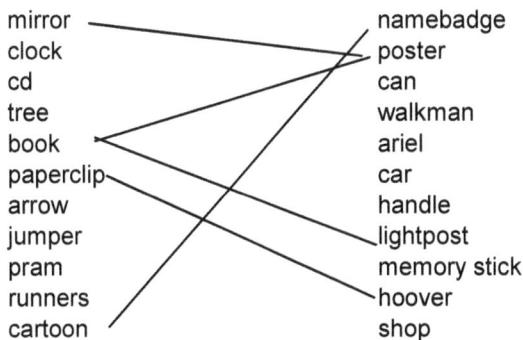

mirror	namebadge
clock	poster
cd	can
tree	walkman
book	ariel
paperclip	car
arrow	handle
jumper	lightpost
pram	memory stick
runners	hoover
cartoon	shop

mirror-poster = poster superimposed
book-poster = popular posters in book
book-lightpost = illuminous ink
paperclip-hoover = magnetic paper clips
cartoon-namebadge = novelty cartoon of person

Another variant also from (Michalko 2001) uses object and verbs from unrelated fields to inspire novel new ideas.

Example:

Bedroom	**Automobile**
Bed	Carries Passengers
Place to sleep	Moves
Window Shades	Heater
Near Bathroom	Different Colors
Sense of Security	Auto Door Lock

Ideas:
Window Shades – Moves: Light sensors to open and close curtains for security reasons etc. if people are away on vacation to give the idea that the house is occupied.
Sense of Security – Auto Door Lock: Master lock in room for whole house

Section Five

Tool # 12:   **Relational Words**

The relational word technique takes an existing pair of words and seeks to add in a relational word (example; "while", "beyond", "down", etc.) to stimulate improvement ideas. Originally conceived by Crovitz in 1970 and described by Van Gundy (1981).

Below is a table of frequent English relational words:

About	Above	Across	After	Against	Along
Amid	Among	And	Around	As	At
Because	Before	Behind	Below	Beneath	Beside
Between	Beyond	But	By	Down	During
Except	For	From	If	In	Into
Near	Not	Now	Of	Off	On
Opposite	Or	Out	Over	Past	Round
Since	So	Still	Then	Though	Through
Throughout	To	Toward	Under	Up	Upon
When	Where	While	With	Within	Without

Source: mycoted.com

Example:

• Break your challenge apart into elements

Example - : Improve the clock radio

Some of the elements of the clock radio include clock, radio, electric power source, light, switch, plastic, design, colour, print, alarm, and timer.

• Select two major clock elements

Clock, Alarm

• Select a relational word and insert it between two problem elements

Clock **while** Alarm

• Examine the combination and write down any ideas triggered

✓ flashing light while alarm sounds
✓ radio sound magnifies during alarm
✓ calls out time during alarm and issues you a challenge to get up

•   Repeat steps two and three and write down your ideas

Electric Power   Print

Electric power **beyond** Print

✓ solar powered clock radio
✓ fan operated chime

- ✓ squirt water jet to wake person up!

Design **down** Switch

- ✓ transparent
- ✓ voice activated turnoff
- ✓ puts you too sleep – build in hypnotic/relaxation music
- ✓ lavender spray capsule at night to induce sleep
- ✓ stimulant fragrance in morning

Tool # 13:   Idea Logbook

"Held in the palms of thousands of disgruntled people over the centuries have been ideas worth millions - if they only had taken the first step and then followed through." Robert M. Hayes

Capturing ideas and sketches in notebooks can be traced all the way back to Da Vinci and beyond. Writing down your ideas is a great way to encourage and increase creativity. Keep an "idea journal". Do this regularly, and you'll start having more ideas while you are writing them down. Research shows that regularly scanning your notebooks stimulates even more ideas through cross fertilisation and word association. Small ideas may normally be forgotten, but by writing them down, your subconscious mind automatically works on them, and could transform them into something valuable. Indeed they can serve as a valuable record if you are seeking to file for a patent. (If you feel an idea has real potential for a patent or copyright, photocopy the page and post it to yourself in an envelope that should remain sealed and dated.) Setting a quota for the number of ideas that you want to come up with, also has a positive effect on the subconscious mind, as it seeks to reach that target!

Idea Logbook Tips

- Carry a small notebook.
- Record all interesting ideas that you encounter from brainstorming sessions, TV, ideas you read about or create. This helps to cultivate an alert mindset.
- Record and divide them thematically in a notebook. Indicate the source of the idea.
- Use the notebook as an idea database to gleam insights when you have a problem.
- Use your mobile phone as an "ideas diary" via recording insights into the "Notes" function or the built in voice recorder. This gives you the benefits of brainstorming whilst on the move.
- Use your idea notebook at stimulating events like training workshops, conferences, or exhibitions. This can "trigger" ideas for a problem that you are trying to resolve. These are usually great occasions to get some "mind space" back and to reflect. Aha! Breakthroughs are commonly reported at business seminars.

Tool # 14   **Brainstorming and Brainwriting**

Brainstorming was developed in by Alex Osborn and published in a book called *Applied Imagination* in 1953. It is a group creativity exercise designed to generate a sizeable number of ideas for the solution of a problem.

"It's too bad that thinking is not a required course in public schools. Not remembering but thinking". Earl Nightingale

Section Five

Traditional Brainstorming

- Arrange the meeting for a group of the right size and stakeholder makeup (usually 4-8 people)
- Write the topic on a white board or chart, where everyone can see it. The better the problem is defined, the better the meeting tends to be.
- Ensure that everyone understands the problem or opportunity.
- Review the ground rules
    - Avoid criticising ideas, suspend judgement. All ideas are created equal.
    - The more ideas the better, if you limit the number of ideas people will start to judge the ideas and only put in their "best" or more often than not, the least radical and new.
    - Free-wheeling. Don't censor any ideas, keep the meeting flow going.
    - Listen to other ideas, and try to use them to stimulate even more ideas.
    - Avoid any discussion of ideas or questions, as these stop the flow of ideas.
- Have a facilitator to enforce the rules and record the ideas.
- Generate ideas - either in an unstructured way (anyone can put forward an idea at any time) or structure (going round the table, allowing people to pass if they have no new ideas).

Wrap up the session. Ideas that are identical can be combined, all others should be kept. It is useful to get a consensus of which ideas should be looked at further or what the next course of action and timelines are.

Issues with Brainstorming

Brainstorming is the most popular idea generation tool. One of the reasons brainstorming is so popular is because of the belief that grouping people together is always more effective than letting participants work in isolation.

The bigger the brainstorming group, the more time group members spend idle and hence there are fewer ideas produced compared to an equal number of people generating ideas independently. Some people are reluctant to put forward "wild" ideas that they fear others will judge them by. There is also a tendency for certain people to dominate the session. Explaining these problems to the group is effective.

Brainwriting can also overcome these drawbacks. In Brainwriting each participant thinks and records ideas individually, without any spoken communication. This results in a vast enhancement in the idea generation effectiveness. The originator of Brainwriting is not known, but it is believed to have originated in Germany.

Here are the steps in a typical Brainwriting session:
- Participants sit around a table and each one gets a sheet of paper with the same problem statement written at the top.
- At the facilitator's signal, each participant has 3 minutes to write down 3 ideas on the sheet of paper in private.
- When allotted time is up each participant passes the sheet of paper to the participant to the left.
- Each participant now reads the ideas that were written by the person next to them and a new round starts. Each participant must again come up with more new ideas. Participants are free to use the ideas already on the sheet as triggers — or to ignore them altogether.
- The group can agree to stop after a fixed number of rounds (such as when sheets come to a full turn around the table).

- After the idea-gathering phase is completed, the ideas are read, discussed and clustered using affinity diagrams to group commonly themed ideas.

By simply writing ideas silently versus speaking them out loud, the number of ideas generated can be amazing. Since ideas are generated simultaneously, participants are continually generating ideas all through the session unlike the one person speaking at a time method of traditional brainstorming. People still get to cross-pollinate and build on each other's ideas. Ideas are also recorded the moment you get them: no ideas are lost while you wait for your turn to speak as in brainstorming. No one gets left out and everybody contributes equally, regardless of personality type or personal agenda. Ideas are contributed in private. There is no fear of being openly judged by other team members. The ideas can be kept unnamed and participants have freedom to be truly wild with their ideas.

Tool # 15   Six Thinking Hats

"Few people think more than two or three times a year. I've made an international reputation for myself by thinking once or twice a week."
George Bernard Shaw

Six Thinking Hats is a powerful technique developed in the early 1980's by Edward de Bono that enables organizations to view a situation from a number of different perspectives. It moves individuals and groups out of their habitual ways of thinking.

Each "Thinking Hat" stimulates a different style of thinking and the team goes through each stage in parallel thus ensuring that all the perspectives are analysed. The following is a top level interpretative summary:

White Hat: The white hat is concerned with data gathering and evidence of past trends etc. It ensures that decisions are fact based and prevents "group think".

Red Hat: This hat takes into account feelings and emotions. Intuitive responses are invited here even if people cannot back up their reasoning.

Black Hat: This hat evokes the "devils advocate" if you like. It looks at a situation and tries to identify weak spots and potential pitfalls in advance.

Yellow Hat: This hat focuses the group on the positive aspects of a situation and of how it might work out. This is especially important if a team meets roadblocks and thorny issues, as it looks for the positive and opportunity in the difficultly.

Green Hat: The Green Hat represents creativity. This is where you can unleash your creative thinking ability to solve a problem.

Blue Hat: The Blue Hat is the facilitation and organising hat, and is concerned with organising the output of the meeting and assigning action plans etc. It moves the thinking along the various hats and makes sure that people don't wander off a particular thinking style. In effect it converts creativity into innovation and concrete progress.

Six Thinking Hats can be used in meetings or individually. A detailed discussion of this great ego busting technique can be obtained in de Bono's book *Six Thinking Hats* (1999).

Section Five

Tool # 16: Mind Maps

Mind Maps were originated by Tony Buzen in the late 1960's. The visual nature of Mind Maps enables you to distinguish words or ideas, often with colours and symbols. They generally take a hierarchical or tree branch format, with ideas branching out into subsections. Mind Maps allow for greater creativity when recording ideas and information, as well as allowing the note-taker to associate words with visual graphics. This graphic technique provides a means to unlock the potential of the brain.

How to Mind Map

- Start in the center of a blank page turned sideways. This allows your brain freedom to spread out in all directions and to express itself more freely and naturally.
- Use an image or picture for your central idea, your brain thinks in images.
- Use colors throughout. Colors are as exciting to your brain as are images. Color adds extra richness to your Mind Map, adds energy to your creative thinking, and is fun!
- Connect the main branches to the central image and connect your second- and third-level branches to the first and second levels, etc. The reason for this is that your brain works by association. It likes to link two (or three, or four) things together. If you connect the branches, you will understand and remember a lot more easily.
- Make your branches curved rather than straight-lined as straight lines are boring for the brain.
- Use one key word per line to give your Mind Map more power and flexibility.
- Use images throughout as each image like the central image, is also worth a thousand words. So if you have only 10 images in your Mind Map, it's already the equal of 10,000 words of notes! (adapted from www.buzanworld.com)

Mind Maps are suitable for:

- Generating ideas
- Problem solving
- Organise/prioritise key concepts
- Using as memory aid:
- Exploring relationships
- Creating associations
- Simplification of complexity
- Note taking

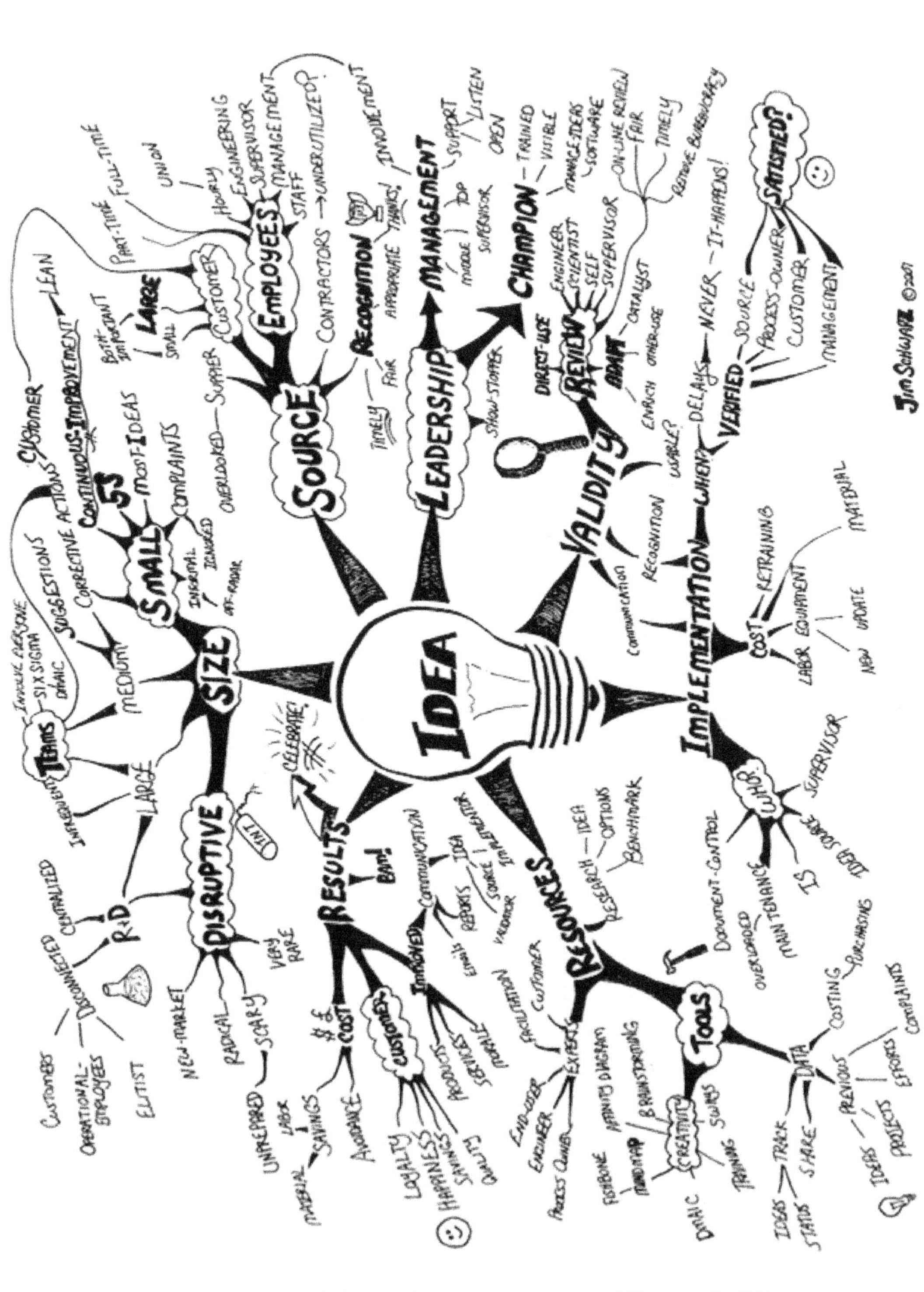

Fig. 4.11 Mind Map (Source: Jim Schwarz of www.tqs-sim.com and The A to Z of Idea Management 2008)

Tool # 17   Concept Fan

The Concept Fan was developed by Edward de Bono and published in his book *Serious Creativity* (1993). It develops the principle of "taking a step back" to get a broader viewpoint. A concept is a high level vague description of an item or situation. The example below tries to capture the thought process behind this method.

Example:

Issue	*General Ideas*	*Concepts*	*Specific Actions*
Litter on streets	(a) More bins	Holding Vessel	Rapid degrading film
	(b) Increase fines	Penalty	Reward use of bins
	(c) Night Control	Care Free	Bulls Eye Litter Price

The issue that is to be solved is to reduce the amount of litter on the streets.

Three general ideas are put forward:

(a) Introduce more bins; the general concept of a bin is that it is a holding device. This sparks the idea of removing the need for a bin like introducing a rapid degrading package film that would dissolve with exposure to the moisture in the air.

(b) Increasing fines, comes under the concept of a penalty and makes one think of how we could reward the use of bins maybe by having a litter warden randomly catching good behaviour of people using bins and giving them parking meter credit etc.

(c) Looks at the idea of how we could tackle the notorious problem of night time littering after night clubs etc., and fast food outlets. How about we had a side show game at litter black spots where people could try and shoot their empty burger bags and cups through a bull's eye or a basketball hoop for a prize!! Far out, but may be a popular and fun way to consolidate the spread of litter.

> *"Thinking is the hardest work of all, and that's why so few of us do it."*
> *Henry Ford*

Tool # 18   Dimensions of Quality (Garvin 1988 & Langley et al 2009)

A product or service can be differentiated using quality dimensions as detailed below. These dimensions include a broad definition of the concept of quality and can be used in the product or indeed any service arena.

1.	Performance	Primary operating characteristics
2.	Features	Secondary operating characteristics, added touches
3.	Time	Time spent waiting, cycle time, time to complete a service
4.	Reliability	Extent of failure free operation over time

5.	Durability	Amount of use before replacement is preferable to repair
6.	Uniformity	Low variation among outcomes of a process
7.	Consistency	Match with documentation, forecasts, or standards
8.	Serviceability	Resolution of problems and complaints
9.	Aesthetics	Relating to senses, such as colour, fragrance, and, fit
10.	Personal interface	Punctuality, courtesy, and professionalism
11.	Flexibility	Willingness to adapt, customize, or accommodate change
12.	Harmlessness	Relating to safety, health, or the environment
13.	Perceived quality	Inferences about other dimensions, reputation
14.	Usability	Relating to logical and natural use, ergonomics

Example:

In the example below we use the Dimensions of Quality to stimulate ideas to:

Improve the Patient Focus & Experience on an Orthopaedic Ward.

1.	Performance:	Patient can reach "call" bell without moving in the bed
2.	Features:	Ensure television is in line of sight of the patient
3.	Time:	Hourly rounding ensures effective pain management
4.	Reliability:	Medication nurse wears a "Do Not Interrupt" red bib so she is less likely to be distracted and therefore make errors
5.	Durability:	Painkiller dosage is effective throughout the entire night
6.	Uniformity:	Wound dressing is standardised and the same across shifts
7.	Consistency:	Charting is done at the bedside involving patient & family
8.	Serviceability:	A no blame culture exists and issues are surfaced freely
9.	Aesthetics:	The roof has Velcro affixed pictures of patients family
10.	Personal interface:	Doctors and nursing staff collaborate seamlessly
11.	Flexibility:	Actively look for improvement ideas from staff, patients and family members

12.	Harmlessness:	Staff disinfect their hands between every patient interaction
13.	Perceived Quality:	Patient meal is served as ordered and is hot
14.	Usability:	Location of toilet light switch is obvious and labeled as such

In service situations, the RATER dimensions developed by Valerie Zeithaml may be useful. These are

1. Reliability: Does the service do what it is supposed to do?
2. Assurance: How much confidence does the customer have in the service provider? What reputation?
3. Tangibles: The physical appearance of the service facility or communication.
4. Empathy: Does the service provider show understanding and the ability to see the issue from the customer's viewpoint?
5. Responsiveness: Is the service provider able to be flexible?

Tool # 19   Subconscious Processing

The power of the subconscious mind and creative genius has been known for hundreds of years. It is the greatest gift you have and a powerful resource for incubating ideas. Your subconscious is the secret archive stored in your mind at birth and enhanced by every waking moment of life. All the great geniuses such as Einstein and Edison knew how to tap into this great power. Your subconscious mind never sleeps. The subconscious mind tends to give you more of what you pay attention to.

- Write a letter to your unconscious about an issue you have been working on. Include all the details about the problem in your letter.
- Ask your subconscious to provide you with a solution to your problem and specify a timeframe when you will be checking in for the solution.
- Seal the envelope. Put it away and go work on another project.
- Most likely at the specified time when you check in on the letter, the solution will have become apparent to you, if not at the exact time, many times it arrives soon after, often when you are completely relaxed or immersed in another activity.

Tool # 20   Slumber on It!

This is another form of tapping into the power of the subconscious mind. Your subconscious mind processes information continually. Before you retire for the night take a few minutes and review a creative project you are working on. Write down the significant words and put the paper near your bedside. Relax and go to sleep. When you awake look at the piece of paper. Oftentimes the solution to your problem will magically appear.

Chapter 9   Idea Management Systems Case Studies

(A) Toyota Motors, Kentucky, USA

Industry: Automotive
Number of Employees: 7500
Contact: Bradley Willis (Former Toyota Group Leader & Assembly Assistant Manager)

What is the Business Imperative for the Idea System?
The purpose of the system is Continuous Improvement of both the People and the Process.

Is there a brand name?
The system is known as the Suggestion System and Quality Circle System.

What resources are involved in running the system?
One person full-time coordinates the system. Training is delivered by Training and Development section of the H.R. Department. One third of a Group Leader & Team Leader's time is allocated to developing their employees' problem solving skills via helping them implement their ideas. Toyota's entire foundation is built on problem solving and teaching one's subordinates how to problem solve.

What is the historical performance of the system?
The system has always being championed by a member of the Toyota family. Suggestion System was developed internally and implemented plant-wide in 1991. Improvements included new Tracking Database and changes to the process for communicating approved suggestions to other departments that eliminates the possibility of payments to team members in different departments for duplicate or similar suggestions. In recent years, focus on continuous improvement has shifted from encouraging individual suggestions to team suggestions in the Quality Circle system that was developed by Toyota corporation decades ago.

Is the system centralised or decentralised?
The system is decentralised, ideas are implemented quickly at the level at which they are raised with the guidance of the work Team Leader and Group Leader as appropriate. Quality Circle improvements are approved and implemented using A3 format within team member's group, but are given plant-wide recognition.

Are there monetary rewards or recognition used? If so what varieties?
There are small monetary award via points based accumulation system to ensure numerous ideas are implemented. Rewards to team members are based on the suggestion's impact on strategic factors of; Quality, Safety, Cost, and Environmental. It has an active recognition program distributing coffee cups, shirts, and hats, etc. 90% of "pay out" is $10 per suggestion. 10% are pro-rated according to amount of $$$$ saved from the suggestion.

Where are the ideas evaluated?
The production system is designed like a living system in that the process demands improvement ideas when it weakens (just like the living needs food). This manifests itself in the "Andon" cord being pulled numerous times per hour. These problems are then solved at the lowest level possible via the associate implementing ideas via problem solving. The Group Leader spends 1/3 of their time mentoring and teaching their employees how to implement their improvement ideas. Senior executives are charged with ensuring that the Toyota suggestion system really works. Their bonuses, promotions, and future employment are tied to serving as "champions."

How is the Idea System promoted?
The system is used in conjunction with Andon to teach problem solving skills. Actually, the entire Toyota Culture is set up for "problem solving". The Andon system itself was a result of problem solving. Therefore, it is in the very fibre/core of everything Toyota does. Filling out suggestion forms is just one more way that Toyota reinforces problem solving. Definition: "Work group, by themselves, will perform systematic problem solving for the work that they do, to the target and goal achievement of the organisation." Participation in Quality Circles is encouraged through team member's Department Management and on the team member's performance evaluations. QC competitions are open for team members to observe and are advertised plant-wide.

How many ideas are received per year?
There are 190,000 + ideas/year captured at Toyota Kentucky. There is a 100% implementation rate.

What are the tangible benefits ($)?
Past published figures have reported that greater than $40 million per year have been saved from implementing employees' ideas at this site.

What are the intangible benefits?
Employees make presentations to company leadership, thus enhancing communication. Employees are empowered to improve and control their own processes. It builds trust and confidence between labour and management. The system improves problem solving and communication skills at the frontlines. Contributing team members have increased job satisfaction and management has relief from responsibility to resolve work process issues and problems.

How long does it take to implement the ideas?
Individual Suggestions are generally completed within 30 days. More complex Quality Circle problem solving projects are completed in 90 to 120 days.

Is there much of a training requirement for the idea system?
It is a normal part of daily work - pulled by "Andon" System, "Need must guide change"... Taiichi Ohno. If you benchmark Toyota you will find: "One system, One voice." How does Toyota make this happen? They create Practical Problem Solving on the production floor. So, the normal part of daily work from the top down and bottom up is to "prevent problems from returning." The suggestion system is a tool to implement the vision. Training on using the Suggestion System and Quality Circle system is delivered in team members' new hire Orientation. Quality Circle Leader training is provided in a regular training schedule for any team member.

Is there software or IT support or was the system mainly manually controlled?
Ideas are posted onto visual boards and also logged electronically. Databases are internally developed for tracking and reporting on Suggestion System and Quality Circle program. The Group Leader and Team Leader/s sign off and coordinate the implementation of the suggestion, in many cases within the normal 8 hour working period.

What are the significant learnings?
1. The primary purpose of the system is to improve the people and the process and to strengthen problem solving ability.
2. The most important factor in Toyota's success is that employees know that their ideas are valued. The fact is reflected in the extraordinarily high participation (75%) and adoption rates (95%) and 100% of the adopted suggestions are implemented.
3. It has resulted in a highly intelligent and dedicated workforce at Kentucky. Employee turnover is less than 5%.
4. The benefit of focusing on producing quality people brings tangible improvements (cost savings) and intangible improvements (trust, skills development, and engagement) for the company.
5. All ideas are valuable. Some save money immediately, but the intent is to improve the current standard and to become more efficient, & safer. Toyota has a saying for countermeasuring: "That which is performed will prevent the abnormal condition from returning." So, if we are having a problem, and a Team Member writes a suggestion to "prevent it from recurring" we pay them for it.
6. The Team Member never loses responsibility for the suggestion.
7. The Suggestion System is structured and focused primarily for the "small" ideas.

(B) Technicolor, Michigan, USA

Industry: DVD Duplication & Packaging
Number of Employees: 1800
Contact: Chuck Yorke (Former Manager, Organizational Development)

What was the Business Imperative for the Idea System?
Continuous Improvement

Was there a brand name?
TIPS (Technicolor Improvement Process).

What resources were involved in running the system?
Norman Bodek held 13 training sessions cascaded throughout all levels of the company.

What is the historical performance of the system?
In 2001 their traditional suggestion program received 250 ideas with 113 of them implemented. Later the goal was two implemented improvement ideas per employee per month. The emphasis shifted away from getting ideas for "what other people can do for me?" to those ideas that people can control and implement themselves.

Was the system centralised or decentralised?
The system was decentralised.

Were there monetary rewards or recognition used? If so what varieties?
Improvement is part of everybody's job description at Technicolor. They no longer required incentives to induce idea generation. Team awards are a much better way to go using items such as T-shirts and pizza parties.

Where were the ideas evaluated?
Ideas were evaluated locally by direct supervisor and led from HR.

How was the Idea System promoted?
A vital success factor was simply to continue to encourage and implement ideas.

How many ideas were received per year?
25, 000 ideas were implemented in 2006.

What were the tangible benefits ($)?
$10 million was saved in first full year.

What were the intangible benefits?
They were increased employee skills and job satisfaction. Employees' personal attitude completely changes when they see that they do have the freedom to participate. They have attained millions of hours without a lost time accident, mainly from listening and responding to employee's wisdom.

How long did it take to implement the ideas?
Normally the ideas were implemented in less than one week.

Was there much of a training requirement for the idea system?
Educate people about the system and take them to places where the system is working well. Norman held 13 classes starting at senior management and cascading throughout the organisation. Be careful of the "it's Chuck's program" effect. Spend time ensuring that each department manager embraces it as their program. Similar to the scenario of - If you're the "Lean Engineer" your dead in the water straight away as you can't introduce this as a way of life alone.

Was there software or IT support or was the system mainly manually controlled?
Ideas were posted on boards at each cell and supervisor logs implemented ideas into a spreadsheet.

What were the significant learning's?
1. Structure: (a) Get the Idea. (b) Act on it. (c) Give quick feedback. (d) Encourage sharing of ideas. (e) Teamwork.
2. The system of management taught in our schools says that workers do the work while managers think and plan.
3. Leadership team asked all employees three types of questions - (a) How can you make your job easier? (b) How can you make your job safer? (c) How can we reduce each of the seven waste types?
4. The beauty of the system was that we were not waiting for Kaizen "Events" to make improvements – they were ongoing every day.
5. Fix employee-management relations first. Management held employee discussion groups and the issues/opportunities from these were posted & resolved within 5 days.
6. Trust is very important - employees will not come forward with ideas if they fear ideas will be used to reduce workforce.
7. A crisis is good to focus attention.
8. Employee involvement is a vital but often missing part of Lean.
9. There was more progress made with the Lean journey in the last two years of the new idea system as had been achieved in the previous six years.

(C) Larsen & Shaw, Ontario, Canada

Industry: Metal Fabrication
Number of Employees: 87
Contact: Allan Kempert (Continuous Improvement Coordinator)

What is the Business Imperative for the Idea System?
The aim of the system is to make Continuous Improvement a way of life.

Is there a brand name?
Quick & Easy Kaizen

What resources are involved in running the system?
Internal: 12 staff part-time. Each department in the company has a leader in the process; an implementation team of 12 people was assembled to look at problems with traditional suggestion programs, causes and solutions. An external company was benchmarked that was successful in this area to enable learning.

What is the historical performance of the system?
Traditional Suggestion System Program prior to 2004. Employee attempts to complete a substantial form, submits to a committee. They disposition it either as approved, not approved, or needs further study. There is a challenge with employee involvement and follow up to employees. The Quick & Easy Process of small self-implemented ideas was introduced to complement traditional system.

Is the system centralised or decentralised?
The system is decentralised.

Are there monetary rewards or recognition used? If so what varieties?
No cash; reward is seeing their ideas implemented! What really stood out to the team was that by asking people to make their jobs easier (to meet their needs), which was the main focus at the out-set of the process, people commented that they felt empowered, listened to, like someone cared, happy about coming to work, no longer parking their brains at the door etc. The focus for recognition is to have management read an idea on the Kaizen board and to go see the employee. The leader then asks about the idea and the employee is engaged to share their idea. In most companies, the only time when a leader speaks to an employee is to give direction or to critique what they have done. Recognition, as practised at Larsen & Shaw, changes this model for communicating with employees (leaves employee with a good feeling).

Where are the ideas evaluated?
Evaluation is done locally by peers and supervisor.

How is the Idea Process promoted?
It is promoted through peers and Supervisors encouraging and asking for ideas daily.

How many ideas are received per year?
There were 1073 ideas put forward in 2006 and of these 1067 were implemented. This represents a staggeringly successful implementation rate of 99.4%.

What are the tangible benefits ($)?
The cost savings are not formally tracked. Two of the IDEAS were tracked for cost savings (to prove a point). The IDEAS took 2 hours to implement and generated labor savings of approximately $6,000/annum.

What are the intangible benefits?
Employee Engagement greatly increased.

How long does it take to implement the ideas?
Normally less than one week

Is there much of a training requirement for the idea system?
A PowerPoint presentation was developed and everyone in the company was trained on the new IDEA process.

Is there software or IT support or was the system mainly manually controlled?
Ideas are shared amongst each Team area. Ideas are then posted at central Kaizen board for all to share. Continuous Improvement Coordinator logs, into Excel spreadsheet, count for employee ideas. Excel charts are shared with teams at month end.

What are the significant learning's?
1. Prior to implementing the IDEA process, the company was running a suggestion program and recognised that it needed a boost. The company appreciates intent of suggestion programs, which in most cases, aims for cost savings. However the IDEA process focuses on the individual and their needs (companies benefit from meeting their employees' needs). As the book (Quick & Easy Kaizen) points out, according to Maslow's Motivational Theory, everyone has needs and at the top level of everyone's hierarchy of human needs, is Self-Actualisation. As self-actualisation depicts, people want the opportunity to create their own identity, to be who they were meant to be, to grow and act out. Quick & Easy Kaizen allows this to happen.

2. The employee completes a simple form that describes the "before" and the "after" state and the "effect" of the improvement idea, receives approval from the leader and the employee implements or coordinates the implementation.

3. Benchmarking is important to "learn from the mistakes of others because we certainly don't have all the time in the world to make them ourselves." After completing the benchmarking, run a pilot of the IDEA process in a small area. After the pilot, implement the process across the company.

4. What really stood out to the team was that by asking people to make their own jobs easier (to meet their needs), which was the main focus at the out set of the program, people commented that they felt empowered, listened to, like someone cared, happy about coming to work, no longer parking their brains at the door etc. The team also noted that the IDEAS coming in were related to not only making people's jobs easier but were also related to safety, set-up, 5S and cost savings. Mahatma Gandhi stated, "Take care of the MEANS and the ENDS will take care of themselves".

5. Create a problem (i.e. opportunity) seeking culture, some people may be so embarrassed that such and such a problem existed and they might let a sleeping dog lie or not reveal what happened. Let's expose the waste without pointing fingers, reap the reward and learn from our mistakes as the only true mistakes are those which we don't learn from".

(D) Ricoh Products, Telford, UK

Industry: IT, Photocopiers
Number of Employees: 610 employees
Contact: Jayne Garner (Continuous Improvement Coordinator)

What is the Business Imperative for the Idea System?
The objective of the idea system is to reduce costs and to promote employee involvement.

Is there a brand name?
The system is called Bright Ideas.

What resources are involved in running the system?
Internally there are four people part time coordinating the system. Externally they are members of ideasUK who provided significant support to establish the idea system initially. This has now evolved to more of a networking relationship as the system is established and matured. Ricoh is actively involved in attendance and participation at the annual national ideasUK Conference. Membership of ideasUK has proved to be an extremely useful benchmarking source for best practice in running idea systems.

What is the historical performance of the system?
The system was established in 2003. In 2008 Ricoh, Telford won the overall private sector award in the annual ideasUK conference for having the best overall idea system of its members and is certified as "Platinum" (highest possible audit compliance) level status by ideasUK.

Is the system centralised or decentralised?
The system is a hybrid of both models. Smaller ideas are implemented in conjunction with the local area supervisor. Large improvements get implemented as Kaizen projects and are tracked and displayed using A3 style project tracking.

Are there monetary rewards or recognition used? If so what varieties?
A £1 token reward is given for all ideas. £25 is paid to the employee when approved by the evaluation committee and further £12.50 when implemented. Also recognition is used; plant walls are widely decorated with plaques of "Idea of the Month" winners and photos with the Managing Director. A visual traffic light system is used throughout the plant (Red, Amber and Green) to make it obvious of each cell status at any given time. These are known as "Roses" and an employee display centre at the Gemba known as "The Rose Garden" displays and recognises implemented Kaizen ideas, and displays the numbers of ideas and savings per time period. This has proved very effective and there is a visitor sign in book to give feedback to employees, to act as another form of recognition.

Where are the ideas evaluated?
The evaluation committee meets weekly to centrally approve rewards and ideas that are routed centrally to committee. Evaluation criteria are:

1. Increase in Quality/Safety
2. Cost Reduction
3. Inspiration/Originality
4. Effort to implement (Did they implement?)

How is the Idea Process promoted?
The key is to keep it current and live and commit resources. Running theme days, for example, "Einstein's Birthday" are good for giving the process a lift and getting extra ideas to be brought forward.

How many ideas are received per year?
There were 1633 submitted in 2006. 2.5 ideas per employee per year is the target.

What are the tangible benefits ($)?
£400K cost savings in period 2003-07 for small ideas. £2.2 million for larger ideas implemented as Kaizen Events from employee initiated ideas.

What are the intangible benefits?
Visual Management through idea communication cards etc, is extremely strong resulting in a very people orientated environment. Employee turnover is down from "120% in early days to virtually zero now". Ideas are shared with sister sites if applicable.

How long does it take to implement the ideas?
The average implementation time is 26 Days (down from original 40 day average).

Is there much of a training requirement for the idea system?
Training is delivered as part of employee orientation in the "Make Waste Visible" module.

Is there software or IT support or was the system mainly manually controlled?
There is an internally developed Lotus Notes system. Three types of ideas are captured: Good Spot (this is to promote observant behavior; an example is the use of senses to detect a bad batch of polymer). Fast Track (supervisor approves and implements locally). Threshold (idea is routed to central evaluation committee for evaluation). There is an offline paper based form system for employees without access to a PC.

What are the significant learning's?
1. Visual Management is a vital enabler; A3 project reporting is effective and simplistic.
2. It is all about the people – engage them and the benefits will follow.
3. System had both traditional and kaizen style traits.
4. Very important to ensure that evaluation team meets every week.
5. Idea sharing is encouraged.
6. "Behavioural Competence" is taken into consideration. This is the process management view of paying attention to both the outcome and how that result was achieved. Example is, did I make an improvement (outcome) and peeve everyone off in the process of achieving this outcome.

(E) DANA, Statesville, North Carolina

Sector: Spicer Off-Highway
Number of Employees: 465 employees
Contact: Jack H. Simms (People Involvement Manager)

What was the Business Imperative for the Idea System?
Reduce Waste and Employee Involvement

Was there a brand name?
Ideas at Work

What resources were involved in running the system?
Internal: 1 staff full-time. Each department in the company had a facilitator team member who worked hand in hand with the People Involvement Mgr.

What was the historical performance of the system?
Process was established mid 1997, with support from Corporate Home Office to involve all people at all levels in the corporation: who knows their work area better than the stakeholder?

Was the system centralised or decentralised?
The system was decentralised.

Were monetary rewards or recognition used? If so what varieties?
In the beginning Ideas were rewarded with cash, which is not the way to run this type of process. As the process was fine-tuned Ideas were redeemed with Dana Bucks, exchanged for Dana Identity Items, such as Hats, Shirts, Jackets, Umbrellas, etc. Then based on the $ amount of Implemented Ideas a % would be put into a draw on a monthly basis and all Implemented Ideas were eligible for the draw.

Where were the ideas evaluated?
Facilitator team members met weekly to approve Ideas and/or Need Review Ideas
Evaluation criteria were:
      1. Safety
      2. Quality
      3. Through-Put
      4. Cost Savings
      5. Customer Relation

How was the Idea System promoted?
Any Idea that was submitted and implemented during the same month and that was related to the topic of that month earns double points. Topics were Safety, Set-Up Time Reduction, Housekeeping (5s), Scrap Reduction, Cycle Time Reduction, Reduction of D.O.A. (defects on arrival).

How many ideas were received per year?
14,457 Ideas were put forward in 2004. The target was 2 ideas per employee per month with 80% Implementation.

What were the tangible benefits ($)?
Savings were viewed in two categories, Cost Savings, & Cost avoidance. Regardless if from Individual or Kaizen Teams, Total Savings for 2004 was $1.1 Million Dollars and Cost Avoidance was $850K.This represented an average $4300 return per employee that year from the system.

What were the intangible benefits?
At the start of this process mid 1997 we experienced 0.3 Ideas Per Person; by the end of 1997 we were at 2.5 Ideas Per Person. At the end of 2004 the implementation rate was 82%. Ideas were shared with sister plants Monthly. At the end of the day what value do you put on People being Involved: Priceless.

How long did it take to implement the ideas?
30 Days

Was there much of a training requirement for the idea system?
On the job training (OJT), as part of Educate the Educator in conjunction with Excellent in Manufacturing.

Was there software or IT support or was the system mainly manually controlled?
From mid 1997 until mid 2003 Ideas at Work process was paper-based, 3 x 5 cards, then later part of 2003 the IT Dept. developed an internal Lotus Notes system. This saved 30 hours per week reviewing Idea cards and routing to proper departments.

What were the significant learning's?
Regardless of where you work at in a company you have Ideas. Our employees away from work run activities in the community, be it civic, or religious, private or public. The Ideas at Work Process allows employees to be a vital part of what's going on,

"A TEAM IS BETTER THAN THE STRONGEST INDIVIUAL".

Section Six

(F) Children's Medical Center Dallas Laboratory

Sector: Healthcare Hospital
Number of Employees: 200 employees
Contact: Jim Adams (Sr. Director of Laboratory and Performance Improvement)

What is the Business Imperative for the Idea System?
The aim is to reduce costs and improve patient care.

Is there a brand name?
Kaizen Board

What resources are involved in running the system?
Kaizen ideas submitted by front line staff are discussed during the morning 'stand-up' meetings. Staff are directed to seek input from supervisors of the area where the change would affect and discuss with co-workers and come to consensus to continue with idea implementation or not.

What is the historical performance of the system?
Children's Medical Center began using the kaizen method in 2007. It's an adaption of the Norman Bodek "Quick and Easy Kaizen" method with elements of the David Mann "Creating a Lean Culture" method where idea cards are posted visually on idea boards in the lab (no suggestion boxes).

Is the system centralised or decentralised?
The system is decentralised.

Are monetary rewards or recognition used? If so what varieties?
A kaizen idea form is completed which shows what the original situation was, what was improved with a picture demonstrating the change and the names of all who were involved in the change. The form is from a template provided by ValuMetrix. There is no monetary award for kaizen ideas but the laboratory technicians feel empowered to affect change in the workplace. Submitting ideas is viewed as a value-added activity and is factored into performance appraisals and merit increases.

Where are the ideas evaluated?
Evaluation is performed primarily by those using the process with help from supervisor, as needed.

How is the Idea System promoted?
Encourage new ideas at shift "stand-up" meetings. This expectation is also part of every lab staff's job description, so the formal expectation is that all staff will not only perform technical tasks, but look for ways to improve the processes they use.

How many ideas are received per year?
There were 68 ideas implemented in the first six months of 2009.

What are the tangible benefits ($)?
Reduced waste in time and motion. Financial savings have not been measured.

What are the intangible benefits?
Employees have a feeling of ownership in their work environment. They feel that their ideas have value and it helps to remove the "robotic" connotation that can sometimes come with insisting on following *standard work* as part of the overall Lean implementation.

How long does it take to implement the ideas?
Small ideas are implemented in days, whilst larger ideas may take weeks.

Is there much of a training requirement for the idea system?
The Idea System is part of new employee orientation & ongoing periodic training is provided.

Is there software or IT support or was the system mainly manually controlled?
No IT needed. Ideas are posted on Kaizen "Wall of Fame" using an available digital template.

What are the significant learning's?
No blaming. Focus on the process. Everyone is expected to look for ways to reduce waste and improve the process.

(G) Baptist Heath Care, Florida, USA

Industry: Healthcare
Number of Employees: Approx. 6000
Contact: Joseph McCrory (Solutions Leader, Baptist Leadership Group)

What is the Business Imperative for the Idea System?
The business imperative is the creation of a system which engages employees by giving them a voice in running the hospital. The idea system encourages all Baptist Health Care employees from top to bottom to feel and participate as though they are owners in the business. Baptist is looking for employee driven innovation at all levels.

Is there a brand name?
The system is called Bright Ideas.

What resources are involved in running the system?
One person dedicates 50% of their time coordinating and overseeing the flow of ideas. Every FTE is expected to implement 3 ideas per year.

What is the historical performance of the system?
The program was established in 1995. The overarching goal of Bright Ideas is to serve Baptist employees and community better. The CEO announced in the year 2000 that every employee from his own level downwards was to contribute one implemented idea per year. Since 2008 that has increased to 3 ideas per employee per year. More than 50,000 ideas have been implemented since the year 2000 with over $50 million in realised cost savings and avoidance.

Is the system centralised or decentralised?
Decentralised, ideas are routed to the participant's direct supervisor.

Are monetary rewards or recognition used? If so what varieties?
People know that their ideas will be reviewed and supported. No monetary rewards are given out. Any idea that is submitted is recognised with a soda or a cup of coffee in the cafeteria. If your idea is implemented, it is recognised with points. Baptist don't rank ideas (i.e. give extra points), all ideas are treated as equal. People thinking about improvement is the mind-set they want to encourage, not the magnitude of the ideas. Employees have the opportunity of cashing in their points for Baptist merchandise and t-shirts etc. This has the added benefit of raising awareness for Baptist in the community when people wear their branded polo shirts etc outside of work.

Where are the ideas evaluated?
Ideas are evaluated for the most part by the idea originator's direct supervisor.

How is the Idea System promoted?
The system is promoted in part by every employee being held accountable by way of having an idea target of 3 implemented ideas per year. The CEO formally announced that people come to work for approximately 270 days per year and everyone is capable of seeing at least 3 ways of coming up with ideas that will improve patient outcomes, save time, improve safety, etc in that period. There is an everyday focus on making today a little better for tomorrow. Supervisors at all levels including the CEO ask at their monthly one to one meetings; "have you submitted your ideas?" This manifests in everyday

incremental improvement. The department where the idea is raised is mostly responsible for implementing the improvement. Idea metrics are in place and reviewed at the operational staff meetings. Every leader is held accountable for their direct staff implementing their 3 ideas per year. Idea spread and sharing across departments is encouraged. The notion of small "just do it" ideas is promoted. A simple example of this was an employee working in the medical records departments who had the simple but elegant idea to reuse the dividers in the medical charts. This resulted in 55,600 dividers not needing to be purchased per year and also it had/has a positive effect on the environment through landfill avoidance and indeed the cost of disposal. Simple ideas really do add up over time.

How many ideas are received per year?
There were 13,881 ideas implemented in 2008 and 13,422 implemented in the first nine months of 2009.

What are the tangible benefits ($)?
During 2008 Bright Ideas contributed $10.5 million in cost avoidance, and $5.5 million in hard cost savings. In 2009 the savings for the first nine months stood at $19.6 million in cost avoidance and $5.1 million in cost savings.

Note:

Cost Savings are actions taken to reduce historical costs. These include ideas that reduce costs based on current expenditure, ideas that reduce the amount of supplies held, energy saving ideas, preventing medicine wastage etc. An example from Baptist is that during the winter months it is dark on entering and leaving work and the lights are left on constantly. Installation of motion sensors at one location saved $1500 per year.

Cost avoidance are actions taken to reduce future costs. These include ideas for process improvements that do not immediately reduce costs or assets but provide benefits through improved process efficiency, employee productivity, and improved patient satisfaction etc for the future.

What are the intangible benefits?
The idea system enhances employee loyalty; Baptist's turnover % is best practice in the healthcare industry standing at 11%. Employee retention is higher as employees are actively involved in the day to day decision making and running of the hospital. Baptist Healthcare's management knows that their employees are engaged through their attitudes on the job and also through the consistently high performance of their annual employee engagement survey. Baptist has been named on the Fortune 100 Best Places to Work for in America for the last seven years. The idea system is not prioritised towards saving money. Maybe the financial results above prove the old adage that initiatives focused on employee cultural goals return far greater financial returns than those that originally started out as cost saving programs! Employees come to work everyday feeling and acting like they own Baptist Health Care.

How long does it take to implement the ideas?
The average implementation time is 30 days.

Was there much of a training requirement for the idea system?
There were no external facilitators hired to establish the system. Time was dedicated to ensure that employees know what good ideas are, and of the power of employee ideas. Examples of past implemented ideas are used as an on-the-job training tool. New employee orientation introduces the idea system and the CEO attends and provides the

expectation that implementing ideas is a part of the job. People at all levels recognise that everybody is expected to contribute ideas and it is the way things are done in Baptist's work culture.

Was there software or IT support or was the system mainly manually controlled?
Bright Ideas uses an in-house developed web based software application. It communicates the ideas status at all stages of implementation to the idea originator. The package is now available for purchase to external organisations (another employee idea!).

What are the significant learning's?

The idea system must be driven from the very top of the organisation and the CEO must be passionate about excellence. Executives must be active supporters of innovation creation and role models on an everyday basis. This role modeling must cascade down to all the department leaders. People are given clear expectations and are held accountable for implementing their ideas. Accountability at Baptist Heath Care is viewed as a two sided coin. On the one hand it can have a negative connotation that there will be punitive consequences if people don't meet their targets. However there is also a motivational flip side; if people do meet and exceed their targets there are recognition processes in place and opportunities for promotion among many other positive developments. Setting the stage for why Baptist is looking for their employees' involvement and ideas is also an important success factor. The idea system is viewed as a commitment by the organisation to inspire employee loyalty and low staff turnover. Cost savings should be emphasised as a fringe benefit, but the potential is fantastic. A well supported and run idea system is a major contributor to making an organisation a great place to work in. There are no bad ideas, the timing just may not be right. Expect some so called "bad" ideas at the outset as people grasp the concept. It has been rewarding for Baptist to share best practice performance with external people. The system has resulted in better services and outcomes for patients. One idea that lead to process mapping of the patient arrival at the Emergency Department identified 24 unnecessary steps from presentation at the front door to triage. This enabled greatly superior care and response to critically ill patients. Another example from the discharge process was ensuring that patients can read and understand their prescriptions etc. This improved the re-admissions rate significantly. Many ideas are self implemented by the local originators with their teams. Time for improvement is made available at Baptist Healthcare because they don't distinguish improvement work from the normal day to day activities. There is a deep commitment to getting better everyday.

(H) Virginia Mason Medical Center, Seattle, USA

Industry: Healthcare
Number of Employees: 5000
Contact: Jennifer Phillips (Director of Center for Innovation)

What is the Business Imperative for the Idea System?
The purpose of the idea system is to support the medical center's Lean Healthcare journey and to enable the creation of a culture of employee-driven innovation. The system encourages employees to contribute towards the removal of waste in their workplace. The idea system also contributes to the business through improving employee engagement and staff retention by way of involving the people on the frontlines in day-to-day decision making.

Is there a brand name?
The idea system is called Everyday Lean Idea system (ELI)

What resources are involved in running the system?
There are two staff members involved in coordinating the idea system. This accounts for approximately 40% of one person's time running the day-to-day requirements of idea processing and general systems work etc. The other staff member spends approximately 10-20% of her time working on strategic aspects of the idea system such as continuous improvement of the system etc.

What is the historical performance of the system?
ELI was established in 2005 with a pilot project, and full implementation was spread out into the organisation starting in 2006. Each passing year has seen changes and general enhancements to the design and also wider participation and improved performance.

Is the system centralised or decentralised?
The system is decentralised; ideas are generally handled at the outset in their originating work group. The supervisor coaches their staff in implementing ideas and they are recognised locally. The ELI support structure is however centralised.

Are monetary rewards or recognition used? If so what varieties?
There is more of a focus on recognition than rewards. Managers recognise employees locally, promoting ideas within the team, public thanks, etc. There are also areas throughout the organisation called department visibility walls where ideas are posted. These serve the purpose of acknowledging implemented ideas and their originators, and reporting on the status of ELIs in progress. The ideas motivate people to get involved as staff see people reviewing the walls and in some cases spreading the ideas to their own work areas. Department newsletters also carry features detailing some of the ideas put into practice. Another level of recognition is given through presenting ideas on a centralised website called the "Idea Supermarket". This is a repository where employees can submit finished ideas, and they get recognition points if ideas are posted here. They can accrue points this way and cash them in for a catalogue of gift items. Recognition is also bestowed through staff feedback on the website if they get ideas from the "Idea Supermarket" and use them into their own local workplaces.

Where are the ideas evaluated?

When employees see problems they are coached by their managers, who evaluate and guide the originator in implementing the idea. There is no central evaluation at this stage. Later if the idea is submitted to the "Idea Supermarket", it is evaluated using quality criteria and shared. The filter for evaluation is set by specifying that small-scale ideas within the individual employee's scope of control are the target. This simplifies the evaluation process and allows for most ideas to be self-implemented by the originator. Leadership encourages people to act on the waste that they see around them that they can control. This has proven to engage staff. They can, however, also collaborate with other departments working on issues outside of their control.

How is the Idea System promoted?

There are no specific idea campaigns run. More and more managers are promoting the system within their teams by setting individual or department idea targets, having contests, using their visibility wall process or putting a "hassle" jar for staff to share ideas about how to eliminate daily work hassles. The system is promoted on the medical center's intranet home page. A different idea example is featured every few weeks to highlight ideas considered most transferrable to other parts of the organisation. This also drives traffic to the "Idea Supermarket" and promotes further idea activity. Part of a manager's role is to be an idea coach; this is specified as part of their leadership remit. This has proven to be a key design principle. Executives do weekly rounding assignments and pay attention to posted ideas on the visibility walls. It is believed that this will provide additional motivation to participate by signalling interest and support by top leadership. The system has grown organically over time and the idea completion level of managers' teams will be a feature of manager performance plans starting in 2010.

How many ideas are received per year?

There is a caveat here in that only ideas that make it to the "Idea Supermarket" are counted officially so far. There are a lot more ideas out there posted on the visibility walls that are only displayed and tracked locally. In the 2005, the pilot year, there were 68 ideas logged in the "Idea Supermarket". In the first ten months of 2009 that figure stands at 350 tested and implemented ideas. The trend is improving with each passing year and as stated above there is much more idea and innovation activity happening at the frontlines than might seem from the "Idea Supermarket".

What are the tangible benefits ($)?

ELIs have taken waste out and the process appears to be positively impacting staff satisfaction in some cases, although a direct correlation to satisfaction and ELI participation has not been measured. A recent analysis undertaken verified that the system is starting to yield the desired results. Savings are not tracked rigorously but snapshots are provided of hard dollar savings from ideas such as reduction of inventory or costly supplies. The biggest savings have been in freeing up labour hours to work on value-added care. Many defects have been eliminated, for example, through more accurate data, mistake proofing of potential safety issues etc. Tracking concrete savings at the organisational level has proven to be taxing. Employees are asked to provide idea results in the most tangible way possible, but the organisation does not expect them to provide data they do not have ready access to, or to provide guesstimates.

What are the intangible benefits?

There have been many improvements in patient services and general communications and hand-offs. Primary causes of several defects have been dissolved. Employee "hassle factors" have been reduced. Also there have been many examples of ideas that have improved patient safety. Employee engagement has also improved.

How long does it take to implement the ideas?

There is not a metric to track the average length of implementation. However, since the focus is primarily on small, quick change ideas within the control of the originator, ideas are usually realised quickly. This can range from between one and six weeks generally. Ideas are approached using the PDCA cycle (incorporated into the idea form). Testing is required to ensure that there are no unintended adverse consequences.

Was there much of a training requirement for the idea system?

Virginia Mason created their training material internally and training has been delivered in an organic fashion, as and where needed. There is also a leadership module being taught to management on the ELI system. There are so many different skills involved in implementing ideas that it is not possible to develop material to cover all the potential skills. These are taught on the job as required to implement an idea. Employees are guided in articulation and documentation of their ideas. The system appears to be helping with better communication and collaboration among staff and departments. Regular team huddles occur at the visibility walls where people talk about ideas and learning opportunities are surfaced and addressed in this way.

Is there software or IT support or is the system mainly manually controlled?

An IT software package has been developed internally, and has evolved constantly over the years. The original practice was paper based only, but this became unwieldy as the system grew and spread to other departments. There are currently discussions in progress to further develop the idea tools to make it more user-friendly from start to finish. This should help with the sharing and leveragability of ideas, especially as the medical center is based at multiple locations across the city.

What are the significant learning's?

1. Don't underestimate the training requirement and the variety of skills that are involved.
2. Healthcare is complex; following PDCA cycles are helpful to mitigate risk and to maintain a systems view of improvement.
3. Spend time with your executive team at the outset and on an ongoing basis to ensure that they understand the mechanism and strategic fit of the idea system.
4. Don't take too lightly the role of leaders; they must really be interested and available to actively champion the process. Action must be taken upfront to support leaders who are overwhelmed with other work.
5. If employees are not supported when implementing ideas they will not contribute ideas in the future.
6. You really do have to be patient with the evolution of the system over the years; constant learning and course adjustment are required.
7. Never forget that "Thank You" means a lot and promotes the system.
8. Spread the system to the wider clinical roles over time, also include physicians.
9. Physicians in leadership positions have started to get involved after "homework" from the ELI leadership module asked for them to go out and coach three people through the idea process.
10. Team ideas (up to 4 people in terms of reporting ideas to the "Idea Supermarket") are encouraged since ideas rarely impact just one person. Some groups have given themselves catchy names. The "REHAB Innovators" and the "Level 12 Problem Solvers" are examples of teams who have completed ideas! There are also informal competitions between some departments to see who completes the most ideas over a specified timeframe. This complements the formation of a fun environment and there are parties held for the winners, etc.

Section Six

It is refreshing to see some of the great potential of Lean now starting to gain widespread adoption in healthcare. Kaizen idea systems have not been piloted as comprehensively as some of the other Lean concepts in a healthcare setting as of yet. Hopefully these healthcare case studies serve as shining lights and will inspire other hospitals to become aware of the power of capturing their employee ideas in a systematic way.

References

Ackoff, R., Magidson, J. & Addison, H. (2006) Idealised Design, Wharton Publishing

Ackoff, Russell (1999), Ackoff's Best: His Classic Writings on Management, Wiley

Adams, J. (1990) Conceptual Blockbusting: A Guide to Better Ideas. Basic Books, 3rd Edition

Amabile, T. (1998) Creativity In Context: Update To The Social Psychology Of Creativity. Westview Press

Ariely, D. (2008) Predictably Irrational, Harper

Armstrong, L. (2002) It's Not about the Bike: My Journey Back to Life.

Baker, K. (2002). Innovation. Management Benchmark Study. Washington, D.C., Department of Energy Office of Science, Air University (USAF) 16.

Barlow, S., Parry, S. & Faulkner, M. (2005) Sense And Respond. Palgrave MacMillan

Bicheno, J (2006) Fishbone Flow. PICSIE Books, Buckingham

Bicheno, J. & Holweg, M. (2009) The Lean Toolbox. PICSIE Books 4th Edition

Bodek, N. & Tozawa, B. (2001)The Idea Generator: Quick and Easy Kaizen, PCS Press

Bodek, N. & Yorke, C (2005) All You Gotta Do Is Ask, PCS Press

Coffman, C & Gonzalez, M. (2002) Follow This Path, Warner Business Books

Collins, J. (2004) Built to Last. Published by Collins

Csikszentmihalyi, M. (2008) Flow: The Psychology of Optimal Experience. Harper Perennial Modern Classics

Davenport, T., Prusak, L., & Wilson, J. (2003) Who's Bringing You Hot Ideas (and How are you Responding)? Harvard Business Review Feb. 2003

De Bono, E. (1993) Serious Creativity: Using the Power of Lateral Thinking to Create New Ideas. Harper Business

De Bono, E (1999) Six Thinking Hats. Back Bay Books

Deming, W. (1986). Out of the Crisis, MIT Press

Dennis, P. (2007) Getting The Right Things Done. Lean Enterprise Institute

Donovan, G (2003). Corporate Culture Handbook. Liffey Press

Drucker, P. (1985). Innovation and Entrepreneurship: Practice and Principles. London: Heinemann.

Dundon, E. (2002). The Seeds of Innovation: Cultivating the Synergy That Fosters New Ideas (Hardcover), Amacom

Garvin, D. (1988). Managing Quality: The Strategic and Competitive Edge. Free Press

Kao, J (1989). Entrepreneurship, Creativity and Organisation. New Jersey: Prentice Hall

Dorothy, L. and Walter, C. (2005) When Sparks Fly: Harnessing the Power of Group Creativity Harvard Business School Press

Fast Company December 2007 Issue

Grunden, N. (2008). The Pittsburgh Way. Productivity Press

Guido, J. (2009). 'Inside Cisco's Search for the Next Big Idea', *Harvard Business Review*

Hall, R. (2006) Presentation at Cardiff University LERC Alumni Event May 2006

Higgins, J. (1994) 101 Creative Problem Solving Techniques. The New Management Publishing Company

Hino, S. (2006) Inside the Mind of Toyota. Productivity Press

Holt, G. (2007) IdeasUK Workbook

Imai, M. (1986) Gemba Kaizen. McGraw Hill

Imberman, W. (1986) The Golden Nuggets On The Factory Floor. Indiana University Horizons, Vol. 29, No. 4, August 1986

JHRA (1992) Kiazen Teian 1, Developing Systems for Continuous Improvement Through Employee Suggestions, Productivity Press

JHRA (1992) Kiazen Teian 2, Guiding Continuous Improvement Through Employee Suggestions, Productivity Press

Kanter, R. (1997) When Giants Learn to Dance. Harvard Business School Press

Section Six

Kelley, T. and Littman, J. (2001). The Art of Innovation, Lessons in creativity from IDEO, America's leading design firm. New York: Currency Doubleday.

Kelley, T. and Littman, J. (2005). The Ten Faces of Innovation, IDEO's Strategies for Defeating the Devil's Advocate and Driving Creativity Throughout Your Organization New York: Currency Doubleday.

Kotter, J. (1996) Leading Change, Harvard Business School Press

Leach, J., Stride, C., & Woods, S. (2006) The Effectiveness of Idea Capture Schemes. International Journal of Innovation Management Vol. 10 No. 3

Langley, G.; Norman, C.; Moen, R.; Nolan, K.; Nolan, T.; Provost, L. (2009). The Improvement Guide. Jossey-Bass

Liker, J. & Meier, D (2007) Toyota Talent: Developing Your People The Toyota Way. McGraw Hill

Lengnick-Hall, M. & C. (2002) Human Resource Management in the Knowledge Economy: New Challenges, New Roles, New Capabilities. Berrett-Koehler Publishers

Mahesh, V. (1993). Thresholds of Motivation: The Corporation as a Nursery for Human Growth, Tata McGraw Hill

Majaro, S. (1991). Managing Ideas for Profit: The Creative Gap, McGraw Hill Book Co Ltd

Mann, Darrell (2004) Hands on Systematic Innovation, IFR Press.

Mann, David (2005) Creating a Lean Culture: Tools to Sustain Lean Conversions Productivity Press

Marshall, R., Talbott, J., & Bukovinsky, D. (2006) Employee Empowerment Works at Small Companies, Too. Strategic Finance, Vol. 88; Issue 3, Sept. 2006

Maxwell, J. (2005) Winning With People. Soundview Executive Book Summaries

May, M. (2007) The Elegant Solution: Toyota's Formula for Mastering Innovation. Free Press NY

Michalka, M. (2006) Thinkertoys: A Handbook of Creative-Thinking Techniques (2nd Edition). Ten Speed Press

Michalka, M. (2001) Cracking Creativity: The Secrets of Creative Genius. Ten Speed Press

Philips, J (2008). Make Us More Innovative: Critical Factors for Innovation Success iUniverse, Inc.

Osborn, A. (1953). Applied Imagination. Scribner

Robinson, A. & Schroeder, D. (2004) Ideas Are Free, How The Idea Revolution Is Liberating People Transforming Organisations, BK Koehler

Robinson, A. & Stern, S. (1998) Corporate Creativity, How Innovation and Improvement Actually Happen, BK Koehler

Robinson, A. (2005) Big Results from Small Ideas. Industrial Management May 2005

Schwarz, J. (2006) The A to Z of Idea Management, Innovation Publications 2nd Edition

Society of Manufacturing Engineers (2004). Liberating and Transforming: Employee Ideas & Lean. SME DVD I

Society of Manufacturing Engineers (2004). The People Side of Lean. SME DVD II

Smith, A. & Krueger, A. (2003), The Wealth of Nations, Bantam Classics

Spear, S. (2009). Chasing the Rabbit, McGraw Hill

Thompson, C. (1992) What A Great Idea! Harper Perennial

von Oech, R. (1998) A Whack on the Side of the Head: How You Can Be More Creative. Warner Business Books

Tracey, B. (1993) Maximum Achievement. Simon & Schuster

Ulrich, R. (2004) The Impact of Flowers and Plants on Workplace Productivity

Van Gundy, A. (1981) Techniques of Structured Problem Solving (Hardcover) Van Nostrand Reinhold Company

Yasuda, Y. (1991) 40 Years, 20 Million Ideas. ET

Zeithaml, Valerie and Bitner, Mary Jo, and Gremler, Dwayne (2009) Service Marketing, 5th edition, McGraw Hill

Appendix I
Interviews with Idea Management Experts

Four eminent experts in the field of Idea Management were interviewed to add some closing thoughts and nuggets of wisdom on the process of tapping into employee ideas.

The following professionals contribute some significant learning's below:

Alan Robinson
Jim Schwarz
Chuck Yorke
Bernie Sander

Alan Robinson

Co-Author of "Corporate Creativity" & "Ideas Are Free".
Website: www.ideasarefree.com

The main points from Alan's conversation are summarised below:

"Much of the success of idea systems to-day belongs to the Training Within Industry (TWI) movement from the 1940's and it is great to see this system starting to resurrect in the US lately.

His tactics for establishing an idea system:

- Managers don't appreciate the potential that lies in idea systems. Show data from leading companies of the dramatic returns achieved.
- Go back to school – learn from books and go and see successful idea systems in organisations.
- Write down the idea process flow.
- Suggestion box process is flawed for structural reasons (absence of human involvement) and will never return the potential possible. Companies that get 15-20 ideas per employee cannot be using a suggestion box – to cumbersome.
- Teach about rewards and accountability (track who is submitting ideas). Make idea generation and implementation part of everybody's job – integrate into daily work.
- To engage frontline staff – put in a way that benefits them. Frontline staff are never the problem, so ensure top management are engaged.
- Reduce the "Class System" as in the strips are off! - between managers and frontlines to release the potential of idea systems. Everyone has equal say and status.
- You will see and grasp the intangibles that are holding an organisation back when you have a good idea system in place. It serves as a communication mechanism to management."

Appendix

Jim Schwarz

Author of "*The A to Z of Idea Management - For Organizational Improvement and Innovation*".
Website: www.tqs-sim.com

The main points from Jim's conversation are summarised below:

"Idea Management is an incredible tool to strengthen your organisation via improvement and innovation ideas from your employees. If it gets infrequent facelifts, it is a tool you can keep using as your organisation evolves. It has the ability to open up communication, save money, strengthen customer relationships, identify top performing employees and promote innovation.

Idea systems fail because management has generally not changed how they manage people in 50 years. It is still a very top down approach with the average employee having little input on problems they see in their work experience. These are the people that see the real customer issues or problems with the products/services you provide.

Leadership has tendency to overvalue traditional accounting data (which doesn't tell us what's right - as the saying goes "Not everything that is counted counts and not everything that counts can be counted" Einstein). Accounting tends to look at everything as a cost with cost cutting measures typical solutions. At the same time it can hide the value of a depreciated factory or overhead areas like IT. I have rarely seen cost cutting methods being effective – they are highly political and inefficient. A vibrant idea system can identify and resolve problems when they appear. This can increase revenues or reduce costs long before they become an issue – avoiding debilitating cost cutting measures.

Below are some considerations as a leader when looking at Idea Management in your organisation:

- **Caring About Customers and the Employees That Serve Them -** If you are solely driven by the bottom-line, forget Idea Management. However if you want to drive your organisation by what your customers want and need – Idea Management is a very powerful tool. It aligns employees with customers and finds problems. Customers are happier, more loyal and involved in making your organisation stronger. Employees feel empowered and part of your team.

- **Do You Want a Motivated Workforce or a Lacklustre One?** – High performing idea systems involve over 75% of your workforce. This creates a completely different work environment that not only is much more efficient but more cohesive. Getting this level of participation will take a strong focus for several years but is worth it.

- **Several Key Managers Will Fight Idea Management** – How are you going to handle the 1-3 key managers that really don't want to make your organisation stronger and better aligned to your customers? They may see valid good ideas weaken their powerbase or prefer staying in charge. Are you willing to firmly and positively deal with these few people? I have found these few people can poison your sincere efforts.

- **Getting the Right Leader for Idea Management** – Idea systems generally require someone strong enough to push management to listen to people's ideas. Especially the first few years after implementation. The trend is to start with someone strong but when they move on to give the job to a person that doesn't have the initiative or authority to be effective. Carefully consider the person that is right for the job as well as their future replacement.

- **Becoming a Coach** – Leadership needs to change to the role of coach by mentoring via questions and teaching to draw out the potential of all employees. It is appropriate to become Captain of the Fire brigade when the house is genuinely on fire otherwise switch from fire-fighting mode to fire-preventer and leader/coach. That switchover is challenging for most and some prefer staying in fire-fighting mode.

- **Thanking People** – Everybody likes to be recognised for their efforts. Yet how the rank-and-file employees are recognized is incredibly weak in relation to how leadership is recognised. Idea systems need to recognize participants in a manner that's generous and makes employees feel valued. This doesn't need to be large cash awards since they cause scrutiny to the point that the system falls apart. Sadly, leadership tends to not want to share the profit. Finding a balance of fairly thanking an employee while having management willing to support the reward and/or recognition may be the hardest part of designing an idea system.

- **It Takes Time** – It took decades for Toyota to fully develop the Toyota Production System (TPS), why do organisations try to implement Idea Schemes, Lean or other improvement activities in months or a year? That is impossible.

- **Start With A Scheme That Fits Your Current Culture** – Trying to leapfrog forward to a more modern open culture may not fit and may cause serious backlash and failure of your idea system or innovation efforts. Create a process that fits within your current culture – planning to adapt it in the future as your culture evolves. Below is an excerpt from my book (the "*The A to Z of Idea Management – For Organizational Improvement and Innovation*" on the key leadership phases – design your idea system to fit to the phase your culture is currently at.

Chart: Phases of an Idea Scheme				
Phase	Time Frame	Leadership	Idea Scheme	Comments
1	1-3 years	Hierarchical – Power and information controlled	Traditional Suggestion Scheme – information may not be shared between departments	Ideas routed via formal evaluators. Formal committee may be needed to review ideas to ensure every idea is fairly evaluated. May use cash or points awards.

Appendix

2	2-5 years	Evolving – Larger sharing of information and power	Evolved suggestion scheme or IDEA SCHEME with data more openly shared. Separate innovation IDEA SCHEME for new product and service ideas.	Starting to mentor submitters. Increased use of campaigns to focus idea activity.
3	2-5 years	Facilitating – Start sharing power with employees or teams solving problems	Smaller ideas directly handled by submitters (Kaizen). Submitters more involved in larger ideas.	Investing more training and mentoring in submitters. Competition events for top ideas (given by submitters).
4	2-10 years	Involving – Sharing across management boundaries and to all levels of employees	Innovation/idea portal – ideas are shared. People expected to resolve smaller ideas.	Moving to a pull system for ideas. Focus is on recognition of ideas. Leadership utilises top submitters in setting strategies and goals.

The world is quickly becoming flat. How are we going to compete in a global marketplace? Even ten years ago we weren't worried about China, Korea or India. We need to make our organisations more efficient and nimble. The culture idea systems create are fast becoming a necessity.

My vision is companies in the West will only survive if they truly evolve and listen to their employees and customers to improve and innovate. They can only outsource for so long until they are outstripped by Western companies that have evolved or by counterparts in China or elsewhere. Companies with a traditional management style will survive if all operating costs are lower (e.g., a company based in China) or subsidised by their government. Even these companies will be threatened if competitors honestly apply improvement concepts like Idea Management.

Considering idea management may be your best tool for survival. Consider it."

Jim terms the word "Holistic Innovation". Innovation is a continuum of little ideas been implemented. Hence Idea Systems are part of the innovation drive; others are Research and Development, Patents etc. The term Idea Management embraces all forms of improvement and innovation.

Chuck Yorke

Curator of Technicolor TIPS System (one of the world's most successful idea systems) and co-author of "All You Gotta Do Is Ask" and "Where Is Your Company's Next Big Idea Coming From?: There is no limit to the profits innovation can generate".
Website: www.peoplekaizen.com

The main points from Chuck's conversation are summarised below:

"The safest way for implementation is to pilot the IMS with a single supervisor not companywide. Put in the efforts to ensure that this is a success and then leverage companywide on a phased basis.

Don't label the system as the cause of a particular champion, it must be owned at the frontlines.

It can seem like more work for the supervisor in the short term, in expectation of longer term gains. Time to implement is a challenge as supervisor's incentives and metrics are based on getting the widgets out the door on time. This is where management support comes in to integrate into daily work and remove roadblocks.

It is important not to throw this system at the people, activity such as stakeholder analysis and force fields & other management of change activity helps gain buy-in. However, learn as you go - the more structure you put in at the start runs the opportunity of losing creativity.

Use "Daily Readings" where managers go to boards and read the ideas. Perhaps there is no need to write all ideas in a small company or service office. Don't post unnecessarily – sharing happens naturally in small firms. Managers must be prepared to lose some control - we can't all think of everything. The following is so true - "the well never runs dry of ideas."

Let people decide what number they will contribute each month – in any case it is more than you were getting anyway. Make sure that the ideas are sound in terms of safety, delivery and quality. Fit the system to suit your existing culture – don't set out to change the culture from the outset. Fit the tools into the existing culture; that is, let the ideas be the pull for the various problem solving and creativity tools. For example if people already understand the process; maybe process mapping is not the tool to use.

The objective is to get everyone thinking about improvement ideas. Encourage small intangibles because that's the way we want people to think (about continual improvement). Constantly invigorate and keep the conversation alive and system in front of people. Technicolor got 25,000 ideas each year for the last two years.

The award is "money (token) in the bucket for each idea and when target is met give a team award which is ok to do".

Ideas are not all self-implemented. Some require skilled tradesmen and some people are not authorized to use certain hazardous equipment such as drills and power-saws etc. Approx. 50% are self implemented by the originator and/or their work team and for the remainder the originator supports implementation with support departments etc."

Appendix

Bernie Sander

Author of "A Wake-UP Call for Idea Champions" and "The Best of Bernie".
Website: www.innovationtransfer.com

The main points from Bernie's conversation are summarised below:

"Approx. 70% of people are not skilled in writing their ideas. The supervisor or facilitator should help them articulate these verbally. They cannot express them but know the solution. Also 70% of frontline associates are never asked, so go and actively look for solutions.

Where do companies get the time to implement? – If there are 100 ideas in the pipeline – take a quick look at each and roughly determine ROI. Another understated area is promotion and selling the potential of the process to ensure it is adequately supported. There is as much potential in the office for improvement – include it in the system to cultivate buy-in. Metrics help to provide a focus for time allotment. Use metrics such as: Benefit Rate, Implementation Rate, Profit Backlog (lost opportunity by not implementing ideas in the queue), and Participation Rate to monitor, grow and sustain the system. Bernie wishes it was called problem management rather than idea management to improve management focus. A screening process is effective for prioritizing time – Clint Eastwood analogy of the good, the bad, and the ugly. Use "Locus of Control" approach that you can effect locally – go or no-go. Implement ideas that are within your circle of influence as a normal part of day to day business. For larger ideas get other people together in a room from effected cross functional areas. Use business strategy for decision making. Don't pass idea on to lie in a queue for someone to get to.

Ask people for ideas on issues that continually bother them, throws money away, tools, and wastage activities. Bernie's approach to starting is to facilitate on the shop/office floor and create an environment where people are asked for their ideas.

Other key success factors are senior management support and active involvement and that the system is linked to the organizational strategy. All thinking has got be about the end user (first principle of Lean!). Embed the system in the Balanced Scorecard. Integrate your system terminology into the language already used in the house. Management must be held accountable for the system – it is not a nice to do bolt on. The owner of each process has got to be the driver. Train local facilitators and idea coaches. Have a succession plan to sustain if people change roles.

People can't think of process improvement ideas when the area resembles a place form the middle ages – deal with basics of good working environment and respect for people first, ideas regarding drinking fountains, annoyances, tidiness, tools, and chairs etc will be the first to come prior to getting really amazing process improvement ideas. 80% of ideas can be locally implemented.

Recognise behaviours for achieving the results along with the results themselves (process management). Points based systems for encouragement of multiple ideas that can be exchanged for merchandise when predetermined point levels have been met, are more effective than cash.

The traditional suggestions scheme is a push process. You sent you ideas to a central area, where evaluators who perhaps are not passionate about your idea, or are overwhelmed already with work, are asked to make a decision and coordinate implementation. The evolved idea system is to use a pull system where the enthusiastic originator gets directly involved and either brings their idea to realisation or oversees the completion of the idea.

It is a good idea to have a strategic centralised steering office where multiple local tactical decentralised systems are established. This ensures consistency of approach and coordinated leveraging."

Closing Comment

Nobody said it was going to be easy, but is anything worth having, ever easy? The question is, does the opportunity that lies before you excite you? If it does and it should, we leave on the same note as the last sentence in chapter one - so, let us begin...

Appendix II

Category	No Evidence	Some Evidence	Strong Evidence	Points
Research				
Are we networking with other well performing IMS's and acting on learning's?				
Have we conducted staff surveys, analysed, and responded to feedback?				
Do we involve trade union(s) in the IMS?				
Are we holding targeted Focus Groups with all stakeholders to capture feedback and action?				
Are we setting, measuring, and achieving organisation objectives?				
Are we aligning the IMS with existing initiatives?				
Administration & Evaluation				
Do the supervisors have sufficient time to consider ideas put forward?				
Is the evaluation role formally part of their job?				
Do employees receive an implementation decision within 24 hours?				
Does the originator implement the idea or coordinate the implementation?				
Are there good open communication lines?				
Do we ask for IMS feedback regularly?				
Are responses to ideas detailed and tactful?				
Are we giving recognition to key role evaluator's play?				
Rewards (if applicable)				
Do we give recognition for non-financial savings?				
Should we be thinking of an "Idea of the Year Program"?				
Are we considering impact on areas that have low scope to submit ideas as with large savings?				
Is paying cash focussing our staff too much on larger ideas?				
Recognition				
Are we been creative in the way we recognise implemented and non implemented ideas?				
Is recognition given visibly?				
Do we have recognition events?				
Do senior managers always give recognition?				
Do we gain publicity both internally and externally?				
Have we considered award dinners hosted by the site manager?				
Budget				
Are we calculating and publishing the annual return on investment?				
Is the budget reviewed annually to ensure that it is sufficient?				
Are we properly managing and monitoring the budget spending?				
Does the IMS feature in the annual report and accounts?				

IMS Accreditation Audit Part I (Source: adapted from Holt 2007)

Category	No Evidence	Some Evidence	Strong Evidence	Points
Objectives				
Do we publish our objectives?				
Are we properly monitoring them?				
Do we set challenging improvement objectives year on year?				
Management Commitment				
Do senior and middle (engineering etc) regularly show visible support for the IMS?				
Are they always involved in celebrating success?				
Do they give recognition at every opportunity?				
Is there an Idea Management Office meeting regularly & focusing on continuous system improvement?				
Are senior management represented on the Idea Management Office?				
Eligibility				
Is there a perception particularly by managers or specialists that they are not eligible to participate?				
Have we a strategy for encouraging ideas?				
Have we encouraged senior management to offer ideas?				
Do we encourage team ideas from informal & non-project specific teams?				
Have we considered inviting ideas from customers and suppliers?				
Rules				
Are they brief and simple?				
Are they published and readily available?				
Do we regularly check that they are up to date?				
Do we challenge the rules to make sure that they are still appropriate?				
Have we involved all stakeholders in the reviews?				
Idea Process Flow				
Have we asked staff if they understand the process?				
Has it been updated to reflect staff feedback?				
Do we always follow the process flow?				
Management System				
Do we produce appropriate measurement reports?				
Has a Standard Work Tasks Matrix been developed for the various stakeholders and consensus gained?				
Do all stakeholders follow Standard Work Task Matrix?				
Training Plan				
Is there an IMS Training Plan in place?				
Is there a plan in place for training all key players in creativity and problem solving skills?				
Communication				
Is there a continuous communication plan in use?				
Total Score:	Level of Award			

IMS Accreditation Audit Part II (Source: adapted from Holt 2007)
Scoring

Appendix

There are 55 questions. The following are the scoring and accreditation levels:

No Evidence   = 0 Points

Some Evidence   = 1-5 Points (make judgement depending on level)

Strong Evidence   = 6-10 Points (make judgement depending on level)

The maximum attainable score is 550 Points

165 Points (30%) qualifies for **Silver Award** Accreditation

225 Points (50%) qualifies for **Gold Award** Accreditation

440 Points (80%) qualifies for **Platinum Award** Accreditation

Appendix III

30 Ways to Increase Your Personal Creativity

1. Experiment with some wonderful iphone application programs for stimulating creative ideas. See www.codeweasels.com for details.

2. Plenty of rest leads to a clear and focused mind. And to introduce a creative paradox; exercise routines such as a good workout in the gym releases feel good endorphins and stimulates alertness. Have you ever experienced going into a workout exhausted and leaving the gym feeling refreshed and invigorated!

3. Go outside your normal work environment and be observant of stimuli that you can relate to your problem in a loose way. Alternatively visit a sacred or historic site that fills you with a sense of wonder and awe and reconnects you with your creative soul.

4. Change your daily routines, shave with your left hand, take a different route through your facility, and notice things that you would not normally question. Habit is the enemy of creativity.

5. Keep a notebook (physical or electronic), and record anything that annoys you throughout the day, these are innovation opportunities. Also jot down any flashes of ideas or creative insights. Saved ideas are like money in the bank, they will gain interest – your interest as you look through them to spark even more ideas.

6. Learn how to mind map (see chapter 8).

7. Spend time reflecting and daydreaming.

8. Don't try to press thinking when solving a problem, spend time collecting information about the problem and then sleep on it or take a break and you'll often come back with a solution. This is often termed the "Eureka!" moment as the subconscious keeps processing the issue while you work on something else and "presents" the answer when you least expect it.

9. Learn to mindstorm; begin by writing a particular goal or problem at the top of the page. For example, if you want to increase your income by 50 percent over the next year, you would write something like, "What can I do to increase my income by 50 percent over the next 12 months?" Or, you can be even more specific by writing the exact amount. If you are earning $50,000 a year today, you would write: "What can I do to increase my income by $25,000 over the next 12 months?" The more specific the question is, the better the quality of answers will be. So don't write, "What can I do to be happier over the next 12 months?" That kind of question is too fuzzy for your mind. Be specific, detailed, and focused in your questions and you will find practical, effective answers. Once you have written the question, jot down 20 answers. Let your mind flow freely. Write down every answer that comes to you. Don't worry about whether it is right or wrong, intelligent or foolish, possible or impossible. Just come up with at least 20 answers. Whatever you write, keep writing until you have at least 20 answers. If you get stuck after writing the obvious answers, write about the opposite solutions. Don't be afraid to be ridiculous. Very often, a

ridiculous answer triggers a breakthrough thought that might save you years of hard work. Next, go back over the answers and select the one(s) that seems to be the most appropriate for you at this moment. You will often have an instinct or feeling about a particular answer. It appeals to you for some reason. This is an unconscious suggestion that you are on the right track. Once you've selected the best option, here's a way to double the creative impact of this exercise: Transfer the answer to the top of a new page and then write 20 ideas for implementing it in your life. You will be astonished at the outpouring of creative ideas that flow from your mind through your hand and onto the paper (Tracy 1993).

10. Develop and use your intuition. The key to opening the door to your intuition seems to be self-awareness. Pay attention to the vibes you get off people. Notice coincidences & feelings, particularly if you have a particular decision to make. If you have two choices to a particular situation, toss a coin and notice if the side you picked and the choice you make feel "right". The body also provides vital information about intuition. Make it a habit to listen to what your body says. Ask yourself, "Is my gut giving me a 'think twice' or do I feel uncomfortable around someone?" Dreams too are sources of our intuition and provide answers to our problems. The secret is to remember your dreams, keeping a notebook by your bed is a good way to catch your dreams as you wake up. Before you go to sleep, ask yourself a question regarding a creative issue that you may be struggling with, or for a new product idea in some specific field. If the answer doesn't arrive the next morning repeat the question, every night for the next week, or so until your answer comes.

11.   Don't be afraid of wacky ideas, "if, an idea at first doesn't seem totally absurd, there's no hope for it". Albert Einstein

12.   Look for ways to make a problem even worse, and then turning those ideas around can lead you to a solution.

13.   Think about how someone else might solve the problem, Einstein, Shrek, or Dyson. Using this different perspective can help break you out of your normal mode of thinking.

14. Try and notice at least one new thing everyday, the asset number on the lamp post outside your house, a new spider web in your work area etc, what it is doesn't matter, your training your mind to be alert and opportunistic seeking.

15. Use foreign and even local travel journeys as creative excursions and be alert to their own local trends and ways of life etc.

16. Organise your thoughts on paper and discuss your ideas with someone else to gain a different viewpoint and see if there are any gaps in your thinking.

17. Describe your problem or idea as a metaphor, "It's like….", this can help you view the situation from a different stance.

18. Do the things you love to do, make a list of activities that make you come "alive" and integrate more of them into your life on a daily basis. Likewise observe your pet hates and try to come up with new ideas to overcome these bugs. Observe customers having difficulty with existing products that they are using.

19. Seek unusual connections. If you are looking for the resolution to a problem, make a connection between this and something completely dissimilar. No matter what two objects you find you should be able to find a number of connections between them. Dip randomly into dictionary or thesaurus every day. The more diverse the connection the more the threshold of your thinking is pulled and it's somewhere within this range that you can find the prevailing idea.

20. Exercise creative thinking each day, for most of us our creative muscles have withered from lack of use. The good news is that we can relearn to be creative through regular practice.

21. Try listening to different types of music to stimulate the right side of the brain.

22. Socialise and meet with people that you would not normally come into contact with; this could stir up some dormant insight within you.

23. Write poetry, this is a great creative workout.

24. Have some random items or toys in your office to stimulate creativity. Build a "Tech Toy Box". Use all five of your senses as well when thinking about new ideas and see how we can optimise the idea to appeal to all of our senses, not just the visual and auditory.

25. Still your mind for a while everyday, chill, meditate, or simply take a walk.

26. Nurture your creative thinking by finding unexpected uses for everyday products.

27. Encourage fun and playful wit, seriousness stifles creativity. Keep humorous items at your desk, such as "The Far Side" calendar etc.

28. Become proficient at using creativity tools such as random word provocation, SCAMPER, and attribute listing etc. Search the web for the wide array of tools available that help us break out of our normal mode of thinking.

29. Become intensely curious and especially notice so called failures and seek what can be learned from them or what other uses could they suggest. Also pay attention to serendipity and chance encounters.

30. Pair ideas with action, which is the spark with the fire. Persistency and hard work are the keys to a creative life.

"Experience is a hard teacher, it gives you the test first, the lessons afterwards."

Appendix IV

Creative & Innovative Workplace Survey

The Assessment below is completed at the outset of the culture change program to perform a diagnostic of the current state and to determine the magnitude of the gap that is to be fulfilled in order to realise a culture of creativity and innovation.

1. Is there a strategy for creativity and innovation linked to the organisations general strategy and all employees are aware and aligned towards it?
2. Is there is a deliberate process along with metrics defined for Creativity and Innovation?
3. Have you created and communicated a set of core values and beliefs to foster a creative culture?
4. Do you have a team of dedicated individuals representative of all stakeholders that champion the changes required to sustain innovation?
5. Have you redefined the roles of your company leaders to include responsibilities for the development of a creative culture?
6. Do all employees have goals and targets for creativity and innovation?
7. Does your employee performance review process specify creativity and innovation responsibilities?
8. Are there examples of people in the organisation who have been promoted due to collaboratively demonstrating their creative potential in their day to day work?
9. Does your workforce consist of people who have the ability to approach problems in an alternative manner and/or network in other industries?
10. When hiring new employees, do you look for people who are willing to challenge the status quo and have foresight?
11. Is some slack time designed into people roles to enable them to work on their passions and/or creative projects and resources are allocated to ensure that feasible ideas are brought to fruition?
12. Is there a bias for action in the workplace and all new ideas are acted on with a sense of urgency?
13. Does the organisation communicate success stories to maintain the momentum and enthusiasm of your employees as ideas are implemented?
14. Does innovation continually provide revenue generation and cost savings within your company?
15. Are workshops facilitated that allow for meaningful interaction between new and existing employees?
16. Is the physical workspace designed to foster and stimulate creative work?
17. Does the organisation teach all employees the principles and tools of creativity?
18. The leadership team are customer focused and keep abreast of current and future trends in the external marketplace?
19. Does your company have a recognition system that celebrates behaviour that enables innovation?
20. Are decisions made quickly with little red tape?
21. Is there a high degree of honesty, trust, fun, and transparency in the organisation?
22. Is innovation activity weaved throughout the organisation, and not isolated to specific groups?
23. Does the organisations I.T system support idea capture and sharing and general creative activity within the organisation?

24. Are experiments and controlled risk taking encouraged?
25. Are ideas failures known as experiments and people are not blamed for these learning experiences?

Rating:

If more than 80 percent of your answers (20 of 25) are "Yes", then your company is addressing the challenge of fostering an innovative culture.
If 50 to 80 percent of your answers (12 to 20) are "Yes" or "To some extent", there is more work to be done in order to foster an innovative culture.
If less than 50 percent (12) of your answers are either "Yes" or "To some extent", your company needs to re-evaluate its approach towards fostering an innovative culture.

Appendix V

Glossary

(Of terms not discussed in detail within the main text)

Andon

This is a visual control device frequently combined with an audible alarm that employees on the front lines can activate to signal the occurrence of an issue or problem. Its purpose is to expose and communicate problems as soon as they occur and to kick start improvement work and ideas to solve the issues when they are still small.

Bottleneck

The slowest operation in any process, improving this should be the basis for prioritising improvement work.

Cellular Layout

This is usually a U-shaped layout that enables employees and the product/service to flow seamlessly from one process to another with no backflows.

Changeovers

This is switching from producing/performing one product/task to another. Shigeo Shingo developed the SMED (Single Minute Exchange of Die) to improve this procedure from many hours to typically minutes in many cases.

Common & Special Cause

Common Causes—those causes inherent in the process over time, affect everyone working in the process, and affect all outcomes of the process

- Common cause of variation
- Chance cause
- Stable process
- Process in statistical control

Special Causes—those causes not part of the process all the time or do not affect everyone, but arise because of specific circumstances

- Special cause of variation
- Assignable cause
- Unstable process
- Process not in statistical control

Continuous Improvement

This is an attitude were people recognise that there is always room for improvement in the current state of play. Implementing incremental improvement ideas on an everyday basis is the manifestation of this way of life.

Customer Experience

Customer experience is the sum perception of all occasions a customer interacts with a provider of goods or services, over the period of their relationship, be that a once off or a reoccurring association. See also service blueprint below.

Empowerment

This is giving employees more responsibility, authority, and responsibility for managing the processes and improvements within their local area.

Error & Mistake-Proofing

This is also referred to as Poka Yoke (Japanese) or Fool Proof (this term violates Respect for People pillar). Think of the three pin plug to understand this concept, you cannot insert it the wrong way into the socket. Many processes and products can be designed or modified to prevent, or at least make it difficult to make a mistake.

Failure Demand

Failure demand describes the demand on the resources of an organisation caused by the errors they created themselves in the first instance. The opposite of this is value demand that is concerned with providing the customers the right service they want first time round. Useful distinction as many times large resources are consumed dealing with failure demand in organisations.

Fishbone Diagram

A problem solving tool used to stimulate improvement ideas about the likely causes of a problem. It commonly uses six categories to cluster potential causes to a problem, Man, Method, Machine, Measurement, Materials, and Mother Nature.

Gemba

This is a Japanese term that refers to where the actual work is performed. Lean refers to Gemba as being the place where value is added to a product or service. It is encouraged to conduct Gemba or Waste Walks between management and the frontlines. This fosters relationship building and awareness of waste (also commonly called muda) and improvement countermeasures. This should always be performed with a mentoring mindset and not be used to point the finger and playing off the blame game.

Hypothesis Testing

Hypothesis testing is the process of testing sample data from a statistical study to determine whether it is in harmony with what is known about the sample population.

Inventory

The hard cash and materials invested in by an organisation in order to fulfil customer requirements. This is almost always an excellent initial cost saving opportunity. Inventory should be viewed as $ on a pallet! This includes all forms of inventory, be that raw materials, work in progress, supplies and consumables and finished goods.
The traditional view of inventory costs is that it includes capital cost (the cost of capital or the opportunity cost of capital) and holding cost (costs of the store or warehouse, includ. space occupied, wages, damage, obsolescence (date sensitive), and material handling equipment in the store). Some of these costs are regarded as fixed or overhead by accounts but are directly attributable to inventory. Typical figures used by APICS etc would be a capital cost of 10% per year and a holding cost of 15% per annum, leading to an inventory carrying cost of 25% p.a. The Lean view goes beyond this, in most cases inventory actually involves far more cost: work in progress takes up space on the floor (which not only costs space but also prevents compact layouts which in turn means more material handling and increases communication hand-offs, it may involve activities such as cycle counting and record keeping, the cost of back-flushing and other SAP reporting, it

Appendix

may also involve defect deduction and write-off costs. Most importantly large batches of units/task work against flow, it inflates lead/service time. Real costs of inventory are more likely to be 50-80% of the average holding costs per year. So inventory reduction ideas that don't put your customer at risk are good!

Measles Chart

This is a diagnostic chart that commonly is drawn to show the outline/picture of the product or area and is used to show concentration of defects or similar criteria. Each time the problem occurs its location is marked on the chart.

Moments of Truth

Every instance of contact in customer service between the customer and the service provider gives the provider the opportunity to build their reputation and enhance the probability of customer loyalty. Off course the reverse is also true in that each interaction can also destroy good will if performed poorly. This can be as subtle as the receptionist's tone of voice when first making contact. This is a useful tool to integrate with Service Blueprint mapping to visually define moment of truth points in the service delivery system. Then plan for there positive delivery rather than leaving to chance or individual personalities types. Think of your past call centre experiences etc, to see the opportunity for providing a differentiated service through this approach.

Non-Value-Adding

Any process or event that does not bring a product or service delivery towards the desired experience the customer is willing to pay for. These activities show up in the form of the sixteen waste types detailed in Chapter 5. Ensure that you dig deeper into the underlying cause of the specific waste, as the waste itself is usually a symptom of a deeper underlying issue. Almost all processes when scrutinised under the waste lens reveal that the vast majority of the steps are non-value adding. Yes a problem, and also an opportunity.

Overburden (Muri in Japanese)

This is one of the three lean targets along with waste and variation. Overburden refers to excess load and demands on equipment and people in the workplace and is a major reason for stress and errors in the workplace. This can also induce huge cost to the system if this resource is the bottleneck in the value stream.

Pareto Principle

Pareto Charts reveals that most consequences (or outcomes), come from comparatively few causes; that at least 80% of consequences come from 20% of the possible causes.

This also applies to the general effectiveness in our personal lives, that 20% of the things that we do, are responsible for 80% of our accomplishments.

Process

A process is a sequence of tasks that cooperatively brings about a distinct purpose. As stated above in the non-value-adding section, most processes are ripe for improvement work. Indeed all value is created as the result of a process.

The Pygmalion Effect

This refers to the phenomenon in which the greater the expectation placed upon people, the better they perform. The opposite is also true.

Service Blueprinting Map

A service blueprint is in essence a process map that visualizes a service delivery system. The key distinction between a service blueprint and process map is the addition of the customer in the former. As customers are often involved throughout the service process, they are a central part of the success.

The key elements of service blueprints are customer actions, "frontline" contact employee tasks, "backstage" contact employee actions, and support processes. Each of these components is placed down the edge of the blueprint and is separated by three swim lanes. Delineation of roles and responsibilities and development of a common service goal and alignment building are the aspired outcomes.

Socratic Engagement

Socratic engagement is named after the Greek philosopher Socrates; it is a form of inquiry and discussion between employees based on asking questions to stimulate new thinking and to illuminate ideas.

Standard Work

This is a central premise for all truly successful Lean work. Standard work provides the best way to do work and/or provide a service, and is hence a key knowledge management portal. It should be the basis for all continuous improvement activities. The best practice or sequence of activities that minimises waste is established in cooperation with the people in the work area affected. It ensures that activities are executed consistently with no variation. Standard Work Sheets incorporates procedures, inventory levels, and targeted performance times.

- The standard work chart will visually display the work sequence, process layout, and work-in-progress.

- Will visually display the staff movement for each activity, task, or process

- Will visually identify quality standards, safety programs, and safety concerns, duplication of services, and opportunities for errors.

The principle is to have these tools available at the Gemba (place of action) and to be available to Team Members to write their ideas for process issues and improvement opportunities. The supervisor's role is to act on these assignments from their people and to ensure that the process strengthens and improves everyday. Standard Work for employee's daily maintenance and sustaining role tasks is also widely utilised to hold the gains delivered from improvement endeavors. An example (Idea Management Task Standard Work) is detailed in Chapter 4 for sustaining an IMS.
Helpful Hints
- Videotaping can be used to accurately document a current process. Further analysis with the lean project team requires reviewing the video footage and documenting various steps.

- They are viewed as current known best practice and should be used as improvement targets during kaizen events etc.

Appendix

- They should be posted at the work area and complemented with the Training Within Industry (TWI) J-Programs to train employees.

Takt Time

Takt originates from a German word "takt" which means tempo or beat.
Takt Time is used to harmonize the rate of work to the average level of customer demand and to determine appropriate staffing levels. Takt Time is calculated as follows:

Takt Time = Available Time per Day after breaks /Demand per Day

As a general rule processes should be designed to maintain units of takt time around 50 seconds. This serves as a productivity enabler as there are commonly a few seconds lost due to minor losses etc, for each individual work tasks. A few seconds lost for a takt time of 50 seconds ensures a greater productivity rate than say a takt time of 20 seconds including a few seconds lost. It also improves quality as the employee becomes there own internal customer when they perform a series of tasks rather than handing off single tasks to another person to complete. Longer processing times can also reduce the risk of repetitive strain injuries, and hence safety in recurring operations. The principle of Respect for People also comes into play as employees can cross train and perform more complete segments of work, hence enriching their jobs.

Takt time is a key concept to shave away all the Lean waste types, for example it prevents overproduction (the worst form of lean waste as it causes all others) by fulfilling services and operation to match the demand rate.

Total Productive Maintenance (TPM)

The TPM philosophy embraces 5 key pillars.
1. Continuous Improvement in OEE (Overall Equipment Effectiveness)
2. Maintenance Asset Care (Preventative Maintenance, Equipment Condition Monitoring and Predictive Maintenance)
3. Operator Asset Care (operator involvement in maintaining their equipment)
4. Skills Development (up-skilling through improvement work)
5. Early Equipment Management (equipment designed to exactly match the work tasks)

Value-Adding (VA)

A task is defined as value adding if it meets the following criteria:

- The customer is willing to pay for the task
- The tasks must move the product or service delivery towards the final outcome that the customer requires
- The task is done right the first time.

Variation

This is the great enemy of Lean. Variation in measurement, time, and demand is found in every process from supply chain demand amplification to dimensional variation. As discussed in Chapter one variation is also intimately linked to utilisation level. Learn to distinguish between common and special cause variation and treat them appropriately. See common and special cause variation above.

Waste

(a.k.a. "MUDA" in Japanese) Any activity which utilises equipment, materials, parts, space, employee time or other corporate resource beyond the minimum amount required for value-added operations to insure that the product or service are delivered correctly.

www.ingramcontent.com/pod-product-compliance
Lightning Source LLC
Chambersburg PA
CBHW081535220326
41598CB00036B/6438